A Handful of Purple Sky

A Handful of Purple Sky

My Second Chance at Life

MRIDULA BAJPAI

Foreword by Pramod Kapoor

AMARYLLIS

AMARYLLIS

An imprint of Manjul Publishing House Pvt. Ltd.
• C-16, Sector 3, Noida, Uttar Pradesh 201301, India
Website: www.manjulindia.com

Registered Office:
• 10, Nishat Colony, Bhopal 462 003 – India

Distribution Centres:
Ahmedabad, Bengaluru, Bhopal, Kolkata, Chennai,
Hyderabad, Mumbai, New Delhi, Pune

ISBN 978-93-90924-59-2

This edition first published in 2021
Third impression 2021

Cover Design: Priyanka Sachdev

Printed and bound in India by Thomson Press (India) Ltd.

The author and publisher wish to reiterate that the
references to medical information, diagnosis and treatment in this book
are not intended or implied to be a substitute for
professional medical advice.

For

Chini Mrinalini,

who is all that my heart ever talks about!

Foreword

When I was approached by Mridula Bajpai ji to write the foreword for *A Handful of Purple Sky*, I realised that it is not an easy task to write about a book that reveals such a personal and poignant struggle–Mridula ji's journey through battling a disease that medical science has still not completely won over. Cancer. Not only did Mridula ji fight the illness, she did it with a determination that is rarely seen. Cancer breaks a person, but Mridula ji came back stronger.

Mridula ji's life came to a standstill in the September of 2017, when she was diagnosed with Stage 2b breast cancer. Before that she was leading a normal, healthy life, going about with her responsibilities, both on the personal as well as the professional front.

Being a dedicated daughter, wife, parent, as well as a thorough professional, Mridula ji imparted her duties with focus and determination. Her illness and the rounds of treatment that included eight chemotherapies and twenty-five radiotherapies left her shattered and broken, but she rose from the ashes like a phoenix and faced all adversities with a calmness that was admirable to say the least. No one other than her family knew what she was actually going through, but she knew that she had to be strong as there were several people who were depending on her, most importantly, her daughter, Chini.

Mridula ji's story and attitude towards life reminds me of a quote by American actress Jessica St. Clair, who too is a cancer survivor: 'I remember thinking, "I will do anything and everything I need to do to stay alive for my daughter and make sure this has the least amount of impact on her life." There are a lot of young moms going through this and I want them to know, "Hello, I can do this too!"'

Amy Robach, a well-known American TV presenter, after having recovered, said, 'I am a better parent. I yell less and cuddle more with my daughter. I am a better wife ... I choose my words more carefully, remembering we are what we say. I want to leave every room I enter better than the way I found it.' It is true that going through such intense circumstances makes one look at life with a different perspective. *A Handful of Purple Sky* is full of such little nuggets of wisdom.

Another incident I am reminded of is that of

cancer survivor, Bina Kak, former cabinet minister, Government of Rajasthan, a Bollywood actress, and mother to a boy and girl. Hers is an interesting story that started from around the time her cancer was detected. She had gone to a hospital for some tests. The hospital technician running the tests reacted with an '*Oh tere ki!*' when they realised it was breast cancer. Bina was made to go through many unnecessary tests until a close doctor friend asked her to change the hospital and move to another. She realised that both the hospitals had by far the best equipment, but in the end, it was human talent that made all the difference.

Mridula ji's tale too is dotted with incidents that most of us would never even imagine! Mridula ji is that incorrigible optimist whose glass of life is always full and never empty. The book also talks about the kind of childhood Mridula ji had, the unstinted support she received while studying further and further, her growing-up years, life at Sagar, her appearing for the civil services examinations by chance and eventually clearing it to become what she is today. It talks about her relationship with people along the way, how they motivated her, pushed her to always give her best. Most importantly, it brings out the positive aspects of a life driven by despair brilliantly.

Pramod Kapoor,
Publisher, Roli Books

From the Core of My Heart...

Writing this chapter of my life about how I fought a deadly disease was not easy. I am extremely grateful to Chini, the heart and soul behind this book. Chini, you have always believed in me, dear. Thank you.

Every season has a special beauty. Between September 2017 to February 2018, I witnessed monsoon, winter and autumn. The trees slowly turned from green to a variety of red, yellow and gold. I had survived so many seasons and, finally, I beat the illness. Even though it was the time when trees were shedding their leaves, there was a brilliance about them. This beauty was not a sign of decay but that of the loveliest season. There is some beauty in every falling leaf, and that is how new leaves grow.

I have always believed that 'one must have a dream' that will keep one going. Have faith in God, the blessings of one's elders and the good wishes of dear ones. Most importantly, have faith in oneself, and one can survive everything. Even though tough times come in our lives, they do not remain for long.

I am thankful to God for staying by my side during my suffering. I would have never known my strength otherwise, or what I am capable of. I am convinced now that God does not give us what we can handle, rather, He gives us the strength to handle whatever suffering He gives us. Even the pain and discomfort He sends our way have a purpose.

I am thankful to God for everything in life. I am grateful to Him for all His blessings. In times of extreme distress, I know, 'God, you are always there.'

A lot of people have contributed in many ways, directly or indirectly. Their contributions and encouragement made it possible for me to bring my story to the world.

Thanking so many people for their generosity and kindness is important.

I am blessed to have such a beautiful family–my mother, sister, husband and daughter. Thank you for being around me then and now without having any expectations. I am grateful that you were with me even when I tried to push you away at times.

I am indebted to all the doctors who cured me of the deadly disease and helped me heal myself completely. Healing is a time-consuming process. My doctors inspired me to take care of my body, mind and soul and gave me the courage to never give up.

I am short of words to express my heartfelt gratitude towards all my seniors, colleagues and subordinates in the Income Tax department in Bhopal as well as in Delhi, for holding my hand and giving me all the support and help I needed. I cannot describe such a deep feeling in words.

Friends make ordinary moments extraordinary. I am indebted to all my friends for being there for me. I am thankful to my friend and publisher, Vikas Rakheja, for reposing his faith in my writing and publishing my story. I was touched by his help and kindness during my treatment and this is something that I cannot express in words.

There is so much I want to say to everyone. Many of you know me but were unaware of all that happened during these two years. You might know some near and dear ones who have endured this illness and will be able to connect with me easily. Now that the ordeal is over, all I feel is gratitude towards everyone, particularly people who did not know of my condition but were kind in their own special way.

I want to tell my story to the world. The story of my life is real, and I am the protagonist. Though it may appear unreal to some, trust me, every bit of it is true.

I thank Saurabh Sharma and his friend for typing the manuscript.

I would like to thank Pramod Kapoor for the foreword, Priyanka Sachdev for the cover design and Bidisha Srivastava for the editorial inputs.

This book was scheduled for publication in April or May 2020. The outbreak of the Covid-19 pandemic led to a lot of changes in everyone's life. I am reminded of a quote by Socrates:

'The secret of change is to focus all of your energy not on fighting the old, but on building the new.'

The pandemic brought people closer despite so much talk about social distancing. Women had to work more in the household as no help was available. It looked like a path towards discovery, perhaps that of the self. It became depressing with casualties increasing all over the world, people losing their jobs, schools and colleges shutting down and the economy in doldrums. So many of our friends, relatives and acquaintances tested positive for Corona. The pandemic was beyond our control. To soothe their anxiety and uncertainty, people adopted different methods. I took to finalising my book.

The Covid-19 pandemic and the resulting lockdowns delayed the book-writing process. When I look back, I feel that the long lockdown was not all that bad. It taught us all that by being alone, we were able to know ourselves and could allow ourselves to dream. Great dreams are born in solitude. At times, it became so quiet, and especially during the long summer afternoons, that I would only listen to the beating of my heart.

I also realised that one cannot survive in isolation. It will be illogical to think that one will be able to beat the odds by themselves, without support or help from the outside.

I take this opportunity to thank everyone who came forward to extend a helping hand–my doctor friends, who were always there, my colleagues, my neighbours and my friends. It depends largely on us to decide what solitude, loneliness or being alone is. I did a lot of reading, writing and watched old movies. It was never a punishment.

Mridula Bajpai

One

1 September 2017, Friday

The sky was blue and new rose buds had just bloomed in the garden. It seemed like a normal day. The sun rose around 6 a.m. and I was sure that sunset would also be at its usual time. But, for some reason, nothing appeared normal to me. I had an ominous hunch that my world would not be the same again. The thought that 'things would change' kept coming to me repeatedly. Would it be 'a change' that would not be for good? Well, only time would tell. At this age and juncture of my life, what was to come was quite perturbing.

I woke up at around 5 a.m., a bit earlier than my usual time of about 6. I was feeling uneasy. The freshness and pleasant feelings of a new morning were missing. I tossed and turned in bed for a while. Finally, when it became too boring and uncomfortable, I got out of bed and went about the daily routine and the morning chores in a very mechanical way.

'Since you have been feeling a bit uneasy, why don't you meet the doctor on your way?' Mummy reminded me while I was leaving for work. I was in a hurry as usual.

'*Chali jaungi aaj,*' I replied, picking up my handbag and rushing out of the house. I had been postponing my visit to the doctor for some days now. I decided to meet the doctor in the morning itself. Some important meetings were scheduled later in the day and one could never be sure how long they would drag on. I called Dr Shrikant Jain, a good friend. He and his wife, Dr Abha, have been my friends for many years and were more like family. Their hospital was en route to my office, just a small detour from the main road. When I reached the hospital, the security guard greeted me cheerfully. My daughter Chini was delivered by Dr Abha. We have known each other ever since.

'Doctor *sahab* chamber *mein aap hi ka intezaar kar rahe hain. Seedhe vahin chale jaiyye,* Madam,' said the young receptionist with a broad smile. I walked into Dr Shrikant's chamber, dragging my feet.

'Good morning,' I said.

'Are you OK? What brings you here so early in the

morning?' he asked with genuine concern. 'You are not looking your usual cheerful self,' he added.

'Doctor Shrikant, do you remember that growth or lump kind of a thing on my right side? It seems to be getting harder and bigger. Can you get it checked, please? I hope it's OK?' I asked him with the same dullness which had gripped me since morning.

In 2013, I had felt a small gland-like thing in my right breast. The routine check-ups, including the biopsy, revealed that it was benign. I was told that it could probably be a blood clot or something, and it did turn out to be one, but there was nothing to be alarmed of. I had almost forgotten about it.

'It's better to go in for an ultrasound or maybe a mammography,' the doctor said. He called the duty sister and asked her to take me to the sonography room. Memories from my past, especially not so pleasant ones, came flashing to me while I waited outside for the staff to get the machines ready for my sonography. Was it a bad omen for things to come? I have a peculiar life pattern wherein I keep landing into some problem or the other at regular intervals. When I was writing my civil services prelim examinations, my mother got mangoes to make pickle. I wanted to divert my attention from the overdose of studies. I started chopping the mangoes with a cutter and happily chopped my finger off. It bled so much that I almost fainted. I am in such a hurry always. After I was promoted to commissioner of Income Tax, I went to meet my husband at Jamshedpur. He was posted there at the time. There, while grinding tomatoes in the mixer, I ground my thumb.

Oh God! How much are you going to test me? When will my travails end? I tried to shrug off the unpleasantness and thought of Chini, my adorable daughter.

'Ma'am! Please come in,' the young radiologist said, breaking my chain of thought. I walked in trying to return her smile and lay down on the examination table. She started the scan. In a few minutes her face became serious.

'Is there anything to worry, doctor?' I asked, almost in a whisper, sensing the growing tension in the room.

'Sister Priyanka, Doctor Abha *aur* Doctor Shrikant *ko bulao,*' she told the sister who had accompanied me.

Dr Abha entered the room almost immediately. 'What is it?'

'Doctor, it's a lump and it doesn't appear too good. I think we should go in for a mammography,' the radiologist said, looking at the screen. Dr Abha also looked at the screen.

'Yes, we shall go to the other hospital for the mammography,' Dr Abha said.

'Abha, you have a whole lot of patients waiting for you. I will go myself. Please ring up someone there so that I don't have to wait. I have to pick up Mummy's homeopathic medicines on my way back.' I pretended that everything was normal and behaved so.

By then Dr Shrikant had also come in. 'Should I come along?' he asked sympathetically.

The other hospital was barely 10 minutes away. I decided to go alone. 'Let me not keep you away from the morning rush. I shall go myself. Just request someone there not to delay me much. I am already late for office,' I said calmly, hiding the emotions that were welling up inside me.

Shrikant immediately dialled someone, probably the owner of the other hospital. 'Mridula is a dear friend. We urgently need to get a mammography done for her,' he said as he walked out of the room while discussing the relevant details of the case with whoever it was on the line.

As I came out of the hospital, Dr Shrikant accompanied me, talking to me all the while with the promise that all would be fine. The familiar security guard gave me a crisp military-like salute and rushed to open the door of my vehicle. 'How are you, Perreira-ji?' I asked him as I sat in the vehicle, trying to be my usual self.

'Fine, Ma'am,' he said in his usual courteous tone and rushed to clear the road. I reached the next hospital in about 10 minutes. There was a doctor waiting at the reception. She immediately escorted me to the mammography room.

As the technician switched on the machine, I enquired curiously, 'Is it something serious?'

'Just relax, Ma'am! We are here. Don't worry', she tried her best to console me.

The mammography slide plate was immediately taken to the radiologist's room. I anxiously waited to know what the doctor had to say. These, perhaps, were the tensest moments that I have lived. Time appeared to have come to a standstill. It was evident that something was terribly wrong with me. What was it going to be? *Was it that?* I dreaded to even think of the word. What was happening to me? Would I live to see all my dear ones? Who would take care of my Chini? Mummy had already suffered enough; to have to see this day now! How would I tell them?

The doctor signalled me to come inside his room. There was pin-drop silence. I could only hear my heart drumming loudly. 'Madam, you have three lumps on your right side which appear to be malignant. We will have to do a biopsy before we can come to a final conclusion.'

I was shocked. I couldn't say anything. My voice choked, my feet felt like lead. I felt a sense of despair and wanted to cry, but had no tears to shed.

'Everything is going to be fine. We are all here for you,' he said.

'I am fine,' I somehow managed to whisper.

It was already lunch time. By now I should have

reached home and would have been having lunch with Mummy as she always insisted we should eat together since the office was so close to my house. I am a frugal eater and generally avoid dinner. Breakfast is anyway a rushed affair. I had told Mummy that I would get her homeopathic medicines when I would come home for lunch. I called Dr Shrikant and told him about the mammography report. I requested, 'Can you please get Mummy's medicines dropped home? I am not going back for lunch. I have to go for the biopsy now. And you will have to tell a lie for my sake that everything is fine.' I wanted to postpone the ordeal for my family, at least for the time being.

'Please, don't worry. I am like a family member. It will be unfair to hide anything. Whatever has come our way, we shall fight it bravely,' Dr Shrikant reassured me.

His words gave me courage. I decided to go home. I slowly got into the car and told the driver, '*Ghar chalo.*'

I felt as if my world had come to an end. I was not sure for whom should I feel sorry–my husband, an army officer posted away from us, or my mother who has had her own share of sorrows in life, or for Chini whose mother had been diagnosed with an ailment that may perhaps take her away forever.

And what about me, the brave and bold one who always took on all and any challenge that destiny hurled at her repeatedly at regular intervals.

Losing my near and dear ones had been quite

hard. Memories of losing my father at a young age, my Nana around whom my world revolved when I grew up, and my Mama, Captain K.L. Shukla, whom I had never met and whose stories my mother always told us when we were kids, came flooding back to me. An army officer with 4 Sikh Light Infantry, my Mama-ji had laid down his life in the 1962 war while defending Sela Pass. Am I going to die now? The ominous thought kept playing in my mind as the car sped on the familiar route to home.

Suddenly I remembered Anjali Tripathi, one of our neighbours in Sagar, and very good family friends. Her brother-in-law Dr Harit Chaturvedi is a very famous Oncology surgeon in New Delhi. I called Anjali from the car. 'I need your help, Anjali.' I was almost on the brink of tears.

'What happened, Ruby?' she asked in a concerned voice.

'Anjali, I have three lumps in my right breast which are bad. Was wondering if Harit can help in any way.' I could not bring myself to even utter the dreaded word.

'Don't worry, Ruby, all lumps are not necessarily malignant. However, I shall speak to Harit. He is with Max Hospital. He specialises in breast cancer surgeries.' She tried her best to console me.

'Anjali, I have got both, the ultrasound as well as the mammography done. I am heading for a biopsy now. I know what it is,' saying which I disconnected the call. I could not cry as the driver was with me. I became numb. I had no thought, no feeling, no emotion. I had no inkling that I was alive.

I thought of my husband, Devendra. He had been trying to get a posting to be near the family. I had not yet told him. He had gone out for field firing. I would always pray to God to bring him back safely. Mummy is a very religious person. She always chants mantras and prays a lot. She has also visited various temples and done the parikrama of Goverdhan, near Mathura, so many times to pray for my husband's safe return. Every Wednesday I religiously light a candle and pray to Our Lady. 'How am I going to tell him? How will he feel?' I thought.

These long years we have been with each other, we have set a perfect example of staying far yet being together. We had never served at the same station, except when he took a posting to Bhopal on account of my illness. He would be hundreds of miles away, yet be close to my heart.We did not have internet, Wi-Fi or mobile phones in the initial years of our marriage. Despite the great distance between us, I have always felt his presence around me. The love that I have for him has no limits. We have made a promise to each other, that we will never say 'bye' at the railway stations or at the airports. We always hugged each other and said 'see you'. I fondly remember one of the happiest moments of my life, when we stopped over at the florist shop and he bought all the flowers in the shop for me. The pages of my life had been blank and colourless. It was Devendra who added colour and poetry to them.

Two

Once I reached home, I had to almost drag myself out of the car. It took some effort to press the call bell. Mummy was nearby and opened the door immediately. '*Aaj badi der ho gayi?*' she asked affectionately. Seeing her I broke down.

'What happened?' she asked. Without saying anything more she put her arms around me and let me in. She did not say anything but her touch conveyed volumes of love.

Chini rushed down the stairs. '*Mamma, kya hua? Sab theek hai?*'

I could not reply as tears rolled down my cheeks. I slowly told them what I had gone through since morning. '*Beta*, I am going to get a biopsy done.' Chini was dumbstruck. She insisted on accompanying me. On our way to the hospital, Chini, forever an optimist, kept on saying that all will be fine. God cannot be so unkind to us. The hospital, where the biopsy was to be done, had CANCER HOSPITAL written in bold at the entrance. My heart sank. I generally abhor hospitals. It was difficult to accept that now I was the one who was entering such a place in reality. I had seen such scenes only in movies. The real is often so different from the reel life.

My feet felt like jelly as I got down from the vehicle. We went inside the doctor's chamber.

The same hospital looked so different today. Almost two years back I had come to meet one of the doctors here. He had saved the life of my maid's child and I had come to thank him. For some reason, the doctor also appeared very pensive today. Or maybe everyone was appearing preoccupied to me.

The doctor, on examining the lumps, said point blank, 'They appear doubtful. Madam, it will hurt a bit when we draw the sample.'

All my senses had already turned numb. I did not feel anything, not even pain. The nurse injected Xylocaine before taking a sample for biopsy. 'I am giving this injection to numb the area the sample will be taken from,' she said. Saying this she took the sample. I do not know whether it was Xylocaine or whether my senses were so numb that I did not feel any pain.

'The report will come after 24 hours,' the nurse

said, after sticking thick tape on the area the sample was taken from.

Chini and I sat in the vehicle and proceeded to my office as we decided not to go back home immediately. I hid my tear-filled eyes behind dark glasses. I reached office. I was posted at Bhopal as Commissioner (Appeals) in the Income Tax department. There used to be cases for hearing. Luckily, there were none scheduled today. It was already afternoon. Everyone had started winding up for the day.

I called my able and trustworthy assistant, Pradeep. He must have been wondering where I had disappeared since morning. He came with a bundle of files, probably of the cases which were likely to come up for hearing in the following week.

'Pradeep, *baitho*,' I said in a very composed voice.

He sat down and started to tell me about the submissions filed and the cases fixed for hearing. I patiently heard him out. Once he finished briefing me, I said, 'Pradeep, *kuchh mushkil samay aa gaya hai*.'

'*Kya hua*, Ma'am?' He sounded concerned.

'I have lumps in my chest which are not good,' I replied.

'*Arre, yeh kab ho gaya*, Ma'am?' He was in shock.

'*Sab theek toh ho jayega*, Ma'am.' He tried to console me.

'I may have to go in for a surgery very soon, probably followed by chemotherapy and radiotherapy, as I understand. The biopsy report will come tomorrow.

But the mammography and ultrasound results have already confirmed it,' I said, looking straight at the beautiful painting of the lovely jacaranda flowers hanging on the wall in front of me.

Just then my mobile phone rang. It was Dr Harit Chaturvedi.

'Good afternoon, I am Mridula from Bhopal. Anjali is a very good friend. Doctor, I have lumps in my chest. It doesn't appear to be good. They have got my ultrasound and mammography done. I have also given samples for biopsy today. The report is likely to come by tomorrow.' It all came out in a rush. There was no preliminary greeting.

Dr Harit was very sympathetic. He gave me a lot of courage and support. He said that he would like to see all the reports at the earliest. As requested, my appointment was fixed for Thursday, 7 September 2017. He asked me to come to Max Day Care Centre at Lajpat Nagar, New Delhi.

My fears could not be allayed. I was not sure what the following day would bring. It was not easy to be brave. I remembered the prayer we would recite in school.

'Lord, for tomorrow and its needs I do not pray;
keep me, my God, from stain of sin, just for today.
Let me both diligently work and duly pray;
let me be kind in word and deed, just for today.

Let me no wrong or idle word unthinking say;
set thou a seal upon my lips, just for today.
And if today my tide of life should ebb away,
give me thy sacraments divine, sweet Lord, today.
So, for tomorrow and its needs I do not pray;
but keep me, guide me, love me, Lord, just for today.'

So I decided to live for today. I decided to be brave. The good I had learnt, read, heard and seen in life helped me gain confidence and strength. The most important lesson I learnt was to have faith and courage in myself. I always believe that, 'One only has to do it and one has to fight it out alone.' I decided to do it in order to come out of my illness. There may be hitches, even difficulties, but these were mere hindrances and I had to overcome the hurdle.

I was reminded of the hanging rope bridges over the fast-flowing streams and rivers in the Northeast. You may have seen one. Long back Devendra was posted there. I had crossed them a few times when I had gone to meet him. It's scary to walk over them as the bridge is tied on two ends by a rope. They shake a lot and one can see the river flowing below. As you look down the fear hits you. But in order to reach the other side, one has to walk over the bridge. The trick lies in taking the first step and then walking without looking down or bothering about the hurdles along the way.

I had gone to Arunachal, to visit Sela Pass, where my maternal uncle, Captain K.L. Shukla, was martyred in 1962. Long ago, I had made a promise to my Nana, that I would visit Sela Pass. I could thus fulfil my promise. Devendra took me there. On the way we visited Nyukmadong War Memorial and bridge too. The actual battle with the Chinese took place around bridge number 2.

There were happy memories of our visit to the Kiwi farms, long walks, watching the snowfall. Those happy days are with me forever; they are timeless.

But here I was, in real life, standing on a scary, unnerving bridge. Destiny had placed me at one end of the bridge. But I was not afraid to walk across to the other side. I was sure I could cross it.

Three

The next day, 2 September 2017, I went to meet Dr Subodh Varshney, a renowned surgeon in Bhopal. He had earlier worked in a hospital in the UK, where he had successfully conducted surgeries on cancer patients. He told me about this illness in detail. He allayed all my fears about the surgery.

Dr Harit Chaturvedi, Dr Shrikant and Dr Abha, answered all my questions regarding the illness. My husband and my sister also spoke to some people who had survived breast cancer. All this helped a lot and prepared me for my onward journey.

I was deeply upset with the turn of events in my life. My sister, Meenakshi, is a professor and head of the department of Pharmacy in a university at Mathura. She reached Bhopal the next day by Shatabdi Express. Her arrival gave me a lot of mental support. She was tense and upset but maintained a cool demeanour. Her presence eased out the tension in the house to a large extent.

Devendra also arrived on 4 September 2017. He said, 'Dear, you will recover soon.'

The treatment was to cost a lot. Everyone came forward to help. Even Chini dug out her small savings in order to help and said, 'Babiya, take all this and save my mother.' She could barely speak. She calls Meenakshi, 'Babiya'.

'I am covered by CGHS and it will not be a huge sum. We should be able to manage,' I said. Though at that time I did not even have a CGHS card which is the basic requirement for availing medical facilities. I never felt the need. Till date I had never taken any medical reimbursement in my twenty-seven years of service. The card was arranged later with the good efforts of Pradeep and others. Many of my friends were ready to provide financial help, but it was not needed and we managed on our own.

The next three days in the office were hectic. I continued with my work, sporting a calm smile, as if everything was fine. It was the beginning of the month. All reports had to be sent. Pradeep, who had been posted in my office for almost a year, was very helpful. He managed the entire office work. He also did all the running around to our accounts and CGHS offices to find out about the various procedures and rules. My friend and colleague, Neeraja Pradhan, became a pillar of strength and support. She helped in getting the reference made from an approved hospital in Bhopal to Max Saket, New Delhi.

Devendra, Meenakshi and I left for Delhi on the night of 6 September 2017. I had called Pradeep to the station with some official documents like sanction orders. I had to sign them so that the daily wagers could be paid on time.

'Madam, *yeh* Shirdi *baba ki vibhuti hai, rakh lijiye. Sab theek ho jayega*,' he said. There was so much positivity and confidence on his face.

When we reached Delhi, my friend's car was waiting for us. We went to the army mess, freshened up and immediately left to see Dr Harit. Somehow, I stopped feeling tense and nervous. I knew I was in a difficult situation but I realised that I had to take it head on. Here was the first step to walking on a treacherously long, shaky bridge to cross over to the other side. At the other end was life, my family and my happiness. Where I stood, there was dejection, sorrow and the end of life. Come what may, I had to embark on this journey that was difficult, tiresome, uneasy, but not impossible.

I had to come out of such a difficult situation and here is when one's positive attitude would play an important role. I always believed in God's mercy and kindness. I once again became that incorrigible optimist whose glass of life is always full and never empty.

I was reminded of the story narrated by Sister Imelda, our class teacher when I was in class eighth, about two political convicts. They had been tortured and put through a lot of humiliation. Eventually it appeared that their end would be at the gallows. One night the two of them decided to peep out of the small window on the top corner of the prison cell. The first one looked out by climbing on the shoulders of his friend, 'What do you see?'

'I see nothing. There is desolation and no way to escape. Our end is certain,' he replied in a heavy tone.

Next, the other friend climbed on the shoulder of his friend who was in tears by now.

'It's a beautiful night. There are countless stars in the sky. It's a good omen. I will live to see my grandchildren,' he replied in a cheerful voice.

Eventually they managed to escape. This could be possible because of the optimism resulting out of a positive attitude. One always has to pass through failures on the way to success. The famous quote by Nelson Mandela came to mind: 'It always seems impossible until it is done.'

The visit to Max Hospital, on 7 and 8 September 2017, were the most trying days of my life. To be precise, they were a test by fire. We reached the day care centre of Max Hospital in Lajpat Nagar well in time. Dr Harit had a look at the reports that I was carrying and conducted the preliminary clinical examinations. He said that all was not fine and prescribed further tests and scans. He patiently answered all our general queries but asked us to wait for all the reports before he could take a final call about the further line of treatment.

We reached Max Hospital, Saket, at around 1 p.m. for various other tests and scans. Anjali had arranged all my appointments with the help of Dr Harit's secretaries much in advance.

First, I went to give blood samples for CBC, LFT, RFT and several other things that I had not even heard of before. Next in line was the biopsy. As I had three tumours, three samples had to be taken. This was a painful affair. It was difficult to visualise that this was me, Mridula, who was having to undergo this traumatic exercise. I closed my eyes, prayed and chanted the *mahamantra*. It seemed like an eternity but it was over soon.

An ECG was done, followed by a bone scan. There were machines of various shapes and sizes that made eerie sounds. It was depressing.

I got a PET scan done the next day. Dr Harit came down to the room where the scan was being done and saw the images on the computer. His gesture moved me immensely. He is a truly amazing person and it is impossible to forget his caring attitude. There was a doctor who counselled me before the surgery, explained the procedure to me and assured me that all would be fine. By the afternoon of 8 September 2017, all the tests were over. Devendra and Meenakshi collected all the reports.

On 9 September 2017, I took a flight back to Bhopal and Devendra and Meenakshi resumed office immediately as they knew that they had to take leave at the time of my surgery. In my case, a lot of pending work had to be finished in office as I would be on leave for two weeks for my surgery. I also had to make other arrangements for Mummy and Chini so that they would be comfortable during my absence. My brother Priyadarshi Bajpai had reached Bhopal from Bengaluru while I was in Delhi. He had been with Mummy and Chini during the period of my absence. His arrival greatly helped. My entire family stood with me. 'In times of test, family is the best,' is an old proverb that still holds true.

Was I unhappy? Was I sad? Honestly, I felt nothing. I was a robot who was obeying commands like arranging money, arranging for people to be there if Mummy or Chini needed anything, speaking to family doctors, telling the maid to be available and not to take leave during this period. I told the maid that I was travelling abroad.

My surgery was scheduled for 18 September 2017. I decided to reach Delhi on 17 September, one day prior to the surgery. Devendra and Meenakshi had also planned to reach Delhi the same day. I had an early morning flight. Mummy appeared upset. We didn't speak at all. I had deliberately left without waking up Chini. I didn't have the heart to say bye to her.

The driver came to pick me up. Pradeep waited for me on the way. He was also very solemn. He dropped me at the airport and wished me luck.

The flight from Bhopal to Delhi in the morning was uneventful. I saw a few known faces but I ignored them. I had taken the same flight to Delhi quite often but those were happy occasions. Many a times I had gone to meet my family, friends or to join Devendra. Now the scenario was totally different and I was a mere lifeless object.

After an hour, I landed in Delhi. The vehicle was waiting outside. Picking up my bag I drove straight to the Artillery Officers Mess in Delhi Cantonment.

Devendra was already there. When I saw him sitting there, I don't know what got over me and I started to feel sorry for myself. A cloud of self-pity engulfed me. I know self-pity is destructive. Wallowing in self-pity was not going to help me in my present state. But I found momentary solace in it. Life offers its ups and downs. Blaming certain people, during the course of my life, for the stress they had given consoled me momentarily, but I eventually realised that I had to fight my own battle.

It was only after a while that I could pull myself together. I had to be responsible for myself and my family, I realised. I recalled the words of my friend Vikas Rakheja. He said I had to live for Chini and my family.

I remembered our neighbour in Sagar, Ali aunty. She always said that one should never feel sorry for oneself. No one has ever seen a flower or a bird feeling sorry or wallowing in self-pity. Self-pity defeats one even before the battle has begun. I consoled myself that difficulties should make us better and not bitter. I started thanking God for all He had given me and that helped. I overcame the feeling of self-pity. I realised maybe I had fought a solo battle from 1 to 17 September and perhaps I was tired.

Shelley's 'Stanzas written in Dejection, near Naples' came to my mind.

'I could lie down like a tired child,
And weep away the life of care'

I stretched out on the sofa and cried myself to sleep.

When I woke up, my sister Meenakshi had arrived from Mathura. We all decided to go out for dinner.

Four

18 September 2017, Monday

I woke up at 6 a.m. I was not supposed to eat or drink anything. The overall atmosphere was solemn. We left at around 7 a.m. for a Shiva temple nearby. Our Guruji had said that we had to carry out three 'abhishekas' of Lord Shiva before my surgery. So I bathed Lord Shiva with honey, milk, sugar and ganga jal. Guruji was confident that all the ill effects of the disease would be gone. Perhaps that is why I was cured. The last of the three abhishekas had to be done today. I was fortunate to have been able to complete all three of them before my surgery. After doing the abhisheka and giving sweets for prasad to Pandit-ji, we left for Max Hospital, Saket.

The driver broke the silence, 'Madam-ji, *abhi kuch zyada beemaar ho gaye ho, par jaldi hi theek ho jaoge.*' His words really consoled me.

We reached the hospital and I walked to the room allotted to me. It was a strange feeling. I kept on thinking, 'Is it me? Is it all happening to me?'

The hospital staff took charge. They immediately started the preparations for the surgery. My blood pressure was monitored. A cannula was inserted for all the medicines that were to be injected. My right arm was marked because the surgery was to be done on the right side.

Two nurses came and gave me the dress to be worn for surgery. They asked me to remove all ornaments. I removed my mangalsutra and handed it over to Devendra. Removing my bangles gave me a real feeling of despair. I had never felt so bare in my entire life. The nurses asked me to lie down on a stretcher as I was to be taken to the operation theatre. But I firmly refused. I wanted to walk till I could. They were surprised. They had probably not seen many insisting on walking up to the operation theatre. I came out of the room and started walking, with the two nurses and the ward boys following me with the stretcher. Devendra and Meenakshi also accompanied me till where they were permitted. I reached the operation theatre and finally had to lie down on the operation table. I stopped feeling anything as if I was frozen even before anaesthesia was administered. After the routine preliminary preparations and sterilisation, the anaesthetist, a lady doctor in her mid-thirties, came to me with a smile on her face. She was an ex-Army officer. She injected something and made polite conversation. The anaesthesia started having its effect and I felt drowsy. I don't know when I dozed off.

When I regained consciousness, my throat was aching and parched. I felt as if I had traversed all over the Sahara Desert for months and had not had a drop of water for days.

The nurse put a few drops of water on my tongue but they were not sufficient. I asked for more, but the request was denied. I was then wheeled into my room where Devendra and Meenakshi were waiting. I was transferred to my bed from the stretcher. Meenakshi had put on the Maha Mrityunjay Mantra on her mobile phone. I could hear the holy chants. The nurse who had accompanied me started explaining the instructions to Devendra in a mechanical manner.

I felt a pang of pain shooting through my body. Again a sense of self-pity hit me. What had I done to deserve this? Was I totally responsible for my state or was it someone else? Was it a '*bura waqt*' which would eventually pass? I started reciting the *mahamantra* and felt better. In between my states of consciousness and unconsciousness, I don't recall what I felt but I remember dreaming of my good days in Sagar when I was a child. I spent days reading stories of Rapunzel, Cinderella and books by Enid Blyton. As I grew older, I had moved on to reading Barbara Cartland, Denise Robins and Mills and Boon romances. Various characters from those stories kept coming back to me.

In the evening Dr Harit and Dr Shubham Jain, who had performed the surgery, came to visit me. 'How are you feeling?' Dr Harit asked.

'Doctor, will I be OK?' I asked in a very tired tone.

'Oh, you "are" OK.' He said with a broad smile, emphasising the word 'are'.

'Whatever was troubling you has been removed. There is nothing to worry now. All is well. The surgery has gone off very well,' Dr Harit said.

'When can we go back, Sir?' Devendra asked.

'She can be discharged tomorrow,' Dr Harit said.

'Tomorrow?' All of us, Devendra, Meenakshi and myself were a bit surprised.

'Yes, in fact it is advisable. No point staying in the hospital for more than the time required. Just make sure to follow all the instructions given to you,' Dr Harit said. Bidding me a speedy recovery, they left.

The night was uncomfortable and restless but eventually it ended. From sunset to sunrise, I had seen so many shades and colours of life. Sunrise did give a feeling of hope.

The visit by the counsellor, a young girl from Srinagar, appeared to be a routine affair. She recited the lessons she had learnt by heart and perhaps had spoken to many before. She talked of keeping a positive attitude. Another girl came who advised me on how to do post-surgery physiotherapy as well as breathing exercises during the rehabilitation period.

After the regular check-up, dressing of the wound, a few injections, strips of tablets, the list of precautions to be taken, I was ready to be discharged from the hospital. The peculiar thing was the drain attached to my body that I was supposed to carry for the next eight days till the stitches would be removed.

At last it was time to leave. Devendra requested for a wheel chair, but I refused. Changing from hospital clothes into a dress that made it easy to carry the drain cheered me a bit.

At around 3 in the afternoon, I walked out of my hospital room and took the lift to the ground floor.

'Let us go and have coffee and dosa,' I suggested. Meenakshi, Devendra and I walked into Sagar Ratna. My world had changed perhaps for good. They say that a good surgery is a must in this treatment. The first important stage of the long treatment was over, but a lot was still left.

We sat in the car and drove to the Artillery Officers Mess. It did appear queer moving around carrying the drain on my body. Meenakshi left for Mathura the next morning and I moved on to Alwar with Devendra.

The next seven days in Alwar were quite different. It was a totally new experience living with the drain attached to my body. The contents of the drain had to be measured before being emptied. It was a tiresome and somewhat filthy job. Devendra and, at times, his buddy, did it religiously. A record had to be maintained. I was to be on a regulated diet. Medicines and exercise of the right arm from where twenty-six lymph nodes had been surgically removed were a must. Care had to be taken to avoid lymphedema.

Meanwhile, I received the detailed reports of my biopsy. I discussed them with my doctor friends. I read whatever was available on the internet. I was told that I was at Stage 2b of the disease that had spread to some of my lymph nodes. My tumour was of a very aggressive variety and I would have to take care of my health for the rest of my life. However, the imminent danger was over. I was ER PR positive, which is considered to be a good sign and indicates a higher chance of survival. This facilitates the further course of treatment. I will have to be on hormone therapy for at least five years after the chemotherapy and radiotherapy were over. The hormone therapy has its own side effects though.

I passed the days in Alwar watching TV and most of the times remembering the good old days of Sagar. I thought of my Nana who had been a pillar of support to us since my childhood. I had been a little girl when

I lost my father. I drew inspiration from words that I had read in books or heard earlier. He had lived through tough times in his life and had lost many dear ones. Yet he maintained a positive state of mind.

His inspiring words motivated me. He often remembered the famous quote of Alexander the Great: 'There is nothing impossible to him who will try'. Another of his favourite quotes was: 'Tough times do not last but tough people do.' He often quoted the poet Rahim:

> रहिमन निज मन की व्यथा, मन ही राखो गोय।
> सुनि इठलई हैं लोग सब, बाँटि न लई हैं कोय।।

He believed in it and always followed it. 'Never let your emotions be known to everyone,' he would often say. I had ingrained his mantras. I believe in 'being myself'. I feel that only by being myself can I change the world around me. I am strong and capable. I can stand and deal with any situation. I always remember to count my blessings–every day, every moment and this always reaps profit.

I despise pity and never want to play victim. People unnecessarily and, often insincerely, sympathising with me puts me off. The melodrama that some resort to while offering their good wishes often becomes annoying. I did not disclose my illness to all; only a handful of my close friends, doctors and a few people from my office knew about it. They also kept it close to their hearts and did not break my trust.

My Nana was a great believer in God. I had inherited this belief. Faith in God gave me hope and hope in turn gave me all the strength to endure the pain, both physical as well as mental, and motivated me that I had to come out of this crisis. It is true that one cannot cross the sea merely by standing and staring at it. I started to motivate myself that I will come out of my illness and finally I did.

I thought of the books I had read. I thought of the countless people I had met in my life. There was no one around, like my dear friend Prasanna or Saira aunty or some of my other friends with whom I could have discussed the books. Prasanna Kutti joined school when I was in class eleven. She and I became good friends in university where we both did our graduation.

Books have always been my greatest friends. Reading has always been a passion. When I hold a book, I hold the world in my hands. There are so many good books and I feel that there is so little time. All books appear to talk and I have realised eventually we all end up becoming stories.

Reading books that I had read earlier or remembering what I had read helped a lot in consoling me when I was overcome with dejection. A lot of Hindi books like *Krishna Kali, Pachpan Khambe Lal Diwaren, Rukogi Nahin Radhika, Korja, Urvashi, Draupadi, Yayati* were there on the bookshelf. I did pick up many of them and shuffled through them. I just wanted to go back to my good old Sagar days when all was fine with life. There was no pain, no anxiety, no worries. They were the happiest days of my life.

My neighbour in Sagar and long-time friend, Dr Harsh Mishra, had read out the *Count of Monte Cristo* when I was a little girl of three or four years. I remembered the words that Abbe said to Edmond Dantès: 'Who talks of God and despair at the same time?'

I would often recall my musings, what I had been writing over the years. The words of one of my poems sounded so apt.

> राहों को मंजिल बनाओ,
> न मिलेगी मंजिल, साथ तो होगा।
> इन राहों पर चलते चलते सदियाँ बीत गईं।
> अभी तो कई सदियों तक चलते रहना है,
> तब शायद मंजिल को जाने वाला मोड़ आए।

As a little girl I was very fond of swings, be it in our backyard, park, school, playground or anywhere. I look for swings even today. Whenever I visited the tourist resort in Sanchi I never missed sitting on the swing. My childhood days were the most beautiful days and the best years of my life, full of fun, happiness and joy. It's only now that I realise what magical moments they were.

I miss the swing in the school playground the most. Who knows, maybe the swing also misses me? I still remember those days and I realise what an awesome childhood I had.

My days in Alwar were often spent sitting on the swing in the garden. The swing always gave me a feeling of flying without wings. I liked to go up in the swing. Now was the time in life to push myself to go forward and the swing reminded me of just that. I realised that I was not too old to remember those days and decided to spend a lot of time on the swing.

I loved playing with dolls. The happiest moments of my childhood have been *gudiya ki shaadi* (doll's marriage). It was celebrated with great mirth and fervour. The *baraatis*–the *ladkewale* used to be my neighbours Harsh, Alok and Rajeev. Harsh's sister Kalpana, Meenakshi and I used to be the *janatis*–the *ladkiwale*. The doll and her groom–*gudiya* as well as *gudda*–were both mine. My doll used to get married and, on her *bidai*, used to go to Harsh's house for a while. But eventually the *gudiya* got back to our house along with her *gudda*. Premlal, the house boy, would be busy since morning making all the arrangements. The verandah of the house was decorated with garlands and flowers. Mummy and Chachi, Harsh's mother, would be busy cooking the food. Some food would be cooked in the small utensils that I had. The rest of the cooking was taken care of by Premlal. My father would bring chocolates and toffees in advance to give to the *baraatis*. Kalpana made beautiful jewellery out of chameli flowers.

The *gudiya* and *gudda* were made to sit on the swing and everybody swooned over the beautiful *gudiya*. The guests would get gifts like a dress for *gudiya*, small toy ornaments, chocolates and Poppins. Tripathi aunty would get some cosmetics like cream and nail paint which, eventually, I would end up using. Aunty had once brought a small necklace and a little bracelet for my doll. I still have them neatly packed and kept in the store.

I still love dolls and teddies. I understand the pain of growing up. Life is not just marrying your doll to her prince but it did give joy and remembering those days lifted my spirits. There is still a little girl in me, '*Ek pagal si ladki jise gudiya se khelna aur ghar basana achha lagta hai.*' Holding on to my dolls in my childhood did give me a lot of comfort. My dolls were real and have been my friends. The dolls would still exist in my mind and I believe that in life everything eventually falls in place. Playing with my dolls, taking care of them, dressing them up, that's how I have grown up. I still love them.

I also have a particular fondness for the wandering gypsies in their colourful dresses and black carts. As children we could only watch them from a distance and were fascinated by them. They sold iron utensils and implements. Some were also fortune tellers. The camels, dogs, sheep, cattle and goats that formed part of the caravan were a wonderful treat to the eyes. I envied them. No school, no homework, no drudgery of studies and not having to get up early to board the school bus. What a great life and existence! What freedom! What adventure!

How nice is the gypsy life–not many possessions, travelling under the blue sky, living among the wild flowers, listening to the wind, sleeping under the stars, dancing and singing, and the unbridled spirit. Better to find the freedom or be at home? I wish I were a gypsy. I would always stop to see a stationary caravan. The next day they would disappear. I soon realised that they don't come to stay but to go away.

I had read that true gypsy girls have the spirit of the sun, the moods of the moon and the will of the wind. They ooze freedom. They cannot be tamed. I always longed to be like them. There were so many stories around them. No one knew much about them then. Watching the gypsy caravan pass by the roadside as I sat on the swing in the garden made me introspect. I have always been a happy and carefree person. Now was the time to get back to my old self. Now was the time to find my identity. I was not very sure of my goal in life but I was determined to find it. This made me forget about my illness. The thought that this life is amazing and now I will do what is best for me got me up and going. Thinking of the gypsy caravans lifted my spirits. I realised that life is to be lived at its best even when it appears to be at its worst. There is magic in life and today is the day to start living it.

At times I ask myself if I possessed the wild soul of a gypsy? It is given to us not to just live but to live our dreams even if it means shaking the world upside down a little at times.

I wondered what is in store for me. I tried to smile and console myself that one day life will get tired of upsetting me and soon, once again, I will be able to say, 'Happy days are here again'.

Five

In Alwar there was a jacaranda tree across the road, though it was not in bloom in September. Sitting on the swing I would look at it and recall those happy days when the vacations at my Nana's house were generally spent playing under the tree that would be in full bloom in summer. The purple blue blossoms, with their sweet smell, would be in abundance. There was a small swing on the tree. I would pick the flowers and decorate the doll's house, make garlands and earrings of flowers, or just collect the purple blossoms. I would sit on the swing and feel like I have conquered the world. It was here that I sat and read many books.

The jacaranda tree has been an inseparable part of my childhood, to be more precise of my existence. How many beautiful days I have spent under the purple blooms? Perhaps many actually and countless virtually.

The purple flowers appeared to shower purple rain and always gave an impression of a tree singing. They never fail to uplift the spirits and comfort the mind.

It was under the jacaranda tree that my cousin had often read out *Cinderella, Rapunzel, Snow White, Alice in Wonderland* and other fairy-tales to me when I was a little girl. She had a way of narrating that made everything seem so real. In fact, she is the one who had introduced me to fairy-tales. I grew up believing in Prince Charming and always believed that in the end the princess and her prince charming lived happily ever after. After each story I would ask her, 'Where is Snow White now?' 'What happened to Cinderella and Prince Charming?' She convincingly replied, 'They all lived happily ever after.'

Swinging on the jacaranda tree had brought good luck. I remembered those days when I sat under the jacaranda tree or on the swing. It immediately took away my gloom and despair.

Once again, I became a small girl. I remembered that man who sold cotton candy (*buddhi ke baal*). He would make an appearance once in a while in the Sagar University campus. As a child I would run after him. Beautiful, pink, sugary-sweet dreams he carried in his glass box and rang a bell to announce his arrival. I would start shouting '*Mujhe dilao.*' Life was so wonderful, nice, pink and sugary sweet. I still love to eat cotton candy.

Remembering those fairy-tale, cotton-candy days helped me a lot in dealing with life when it looked bitter and difficult. Do I still believe in fairy-tales? I realised that life is not a trip to the candy shop but thinking of cotton candy did bring sweetness and helped me to look at the bitter life from a different perspective.

The hobble of being alive is rather serious, don't you think so? This is a question everyone in their lives must have asked themselves at some point.

But the incident pertaining to my cousin's life moved me so much and caused immense pain.

The Almighty makes us go through testing times. Someone ends up losing all in life. My cousin is one of those. She lost her friend, husband and child. I can only say one wrong decision, and if no efforts are made to make amends, the entire life is messed up.

All romances never end in marriage. Hers was no exception. I really wonder why life has not been a fairy-tale for her? There was a Prince Charming but he could not come to the rescue of his lady love. The dragon-like destiny was victorious throughout. The person who had narrated so many of these fairy-tales to me lost out on everything in life. In real life, the dragon destiny could not be beaten.

The story of her life that I have mentioned above draws a parallel with Hardy's novel. No one knew that one day life would turn out to be so harsh on her and the person who made me believe in fairy-tales would be in such a situation which is comparable to a tragedy. Someone had aptly said, 'Sometimes the pain grows bigger as a person grows up.'

As for me, I still like to believe in fairy-tales. I pray to God that He must bring back some happiness in her life. It appears difficult for certain equations can never be balanced and they never work.

Thomas Hardy has been one of my favourite novelists. Jude always captivated me and Tess touched my heart. As a research student I had often discussed Hardy with my professor, S. Mallikarjunan. I was the gold medallist in my M.A. course. There was an ad hoc vacancy and I applied for it. I got selected. In my brief career as an assistant professor in Sagar University, teaching Hardy was always a pleasure. The famous quote from Hardy's Tess, 'A strong woman who recklessly throws away her strength, she is worse than a weak woman who has never had any strength to throw away,' always captivated me.

I wish I can close my eyes and travel back to my Nana's old house, sit on the swing under the jacaranda tree and start to feel like Rapunzel or Cinderella in whose life everything falls back in place.

I want to accept fairy-tales to be real even when life was not a fairy-tale for me now. Eventually, all fairy-tales always end on a happy note and there are no sad endings. My life has had so many good moments and, with God's grace, I have to come out of these trying and testing times. Thanks to all those who have been with me and have contributed in the smallest way to make my life happy and meaningful.

I was free and I started to remember so many things. There was ample time. I picked up my old diary where I would write quotes from the books. I opened it and what I saw was this:

> *'Love is a possible strength in an actual weakness'*
> *'I shall do one thing in this life—one thing for certain—that is, love you and long for you, and keep waiting for you till I die.'*

It felt nice reading this and remembering the happy times. I have so much to remember.

Thinking about the happy childhood days made me cheerful. I realised life is too short to be sad. The best time to be happy is today. But I had to be courageous when such an illness had struck me.

On 3 October 2017, we drove to Max Hospital in Delhi. My stitches and the drain had to be removed. What a relief it was! I felt so normal without this baggage. We met the medical oncologist and the radiologist to decide about the further course of treatment, i.e., the chemotherapy and the radiotherapy.

Devendra and I came back to the mess and had a sumptuous meal. In the evening, I went to Gopinath bazaar. The same old bazaar where I had traversed so often in the past. It felt wonderful to be back. I picked up all sorts of things. The next morning we returned to Alwar.

Devendra had served at far-off places. Those were not the days of mobile phones and internet. We communicated through the only means of communication back then–letters and cards. I looked through the old cards and found one, 'You are my today and all my tomorrows.'

I often received huge bouquets on many occasions. I recalled when an army jawan had brought flowers,

'*Memsahab, hamare* Pandey *sahab ne ye phool bheje hain.*'

I sat next to the flowers and clicked a photograph, which was sent to him–Devendra, you have always made me feel on top of the world.

After three days Devendra and I travelled to Bhopal.

It was the day of Karvachauth. Devendra was hell bent that I should not fast. I was not ready to listen to him. I had always fasted very religiously on this day. Finally, I ended up observing a fast for half a day.

We reached Bhopal. It was good to be home. My mother hugged me, she was so relieved to see me. Chini wept. In the evening, we all went to the mall and did a lot of shopping for Karvachauth. Life was returning to normal. Meanwhile, I had to go and finalise my chemotherapy sessions, which I decided to postpone till Diwali.

One important decision that we had to take

was whether to undergo the chemotherapy at Max Hospital, Delhi, Army R & R Hospital, Delhi, or at Bhopal, where I was posted. We pondered over it and took opinions from the doctors also. After considering all aspects, we decided to get it done at Bhopal. For chemotherapy, having a well-settled establishment is a must. We were not in a position to set up a house from scratch in Delhi, that too in this state. Getting the chemotherapy in Delhi and returning to Alwar, where Devendra was posted, was also an option but it still involved at least a day's travel by road. It would have been cumbersome. The chemotherapy protocol, as well as the drugs are standard. Existing facilities in Bhopal are equally good. So we decided to get the chemotherapy done in Bhopal. Now that it is over, I can safely suggest that the chemotherapy should be taken preferably at a place where the infrastructural and administrative support is at its best. The comfort of home and being close to my near and dear ones when the side effects of the chemotherapy are at its worst were important to me.

Before my first chemotherapy session, I had a detailed discussion with Dr T.P. Sahu, my medical oncologist, who very eagerly and willingly answered all my queries

'Is it painful ?' I asked.

'Not really, but the side effects are there–your WBC, LFT, RFT, haemoglobin levels will be monitored to decide if you are fit to take the next dose of chemotherapy,' he replied.

'Anything else, Doctor?'

'Ma'am, there will be hair fall, your mouth will be full of blisters, you will have stomach-related problems, nausea. You have to also watch out for any infection. In case of even slight fever, inform us immediately.'

The thought of losing my hair took away all the courage. I started feeling miserable. Once the hair goes then... I did not even want to think of it. All this scared me. There was a sense of loneliness and increased pain. I grieved alone. There have even been times when I hid my face in the pillow and cried. I soon realised I had no option. I had to overcome all this and move on.

Six

The first chemotherapy session was scheduled on 24 October 2017. In all, there were to be eight chemotherapy sessions at an interval of fifteen days. The interval between two consecutive chemotherapy sessions is generally three weeks. The side effects of the drug are pretty harsh. It takes three weeks for the patient to be physically as well mentally ready to go through the therapy again. However, a more aggressive line of treatment entails having a lesser interval of just two weeks. By the time the side effects of one chemotherapy session are barely over, the next dose is administered. It is absolutely taxing. It really stretches one's will power. While explaining the nuances of the chemotherapy, the Medical Oncologist at Max Hospital, Delhi, Dr Arya, explained the pros and cons of having a 'three-week' vs a 'two-week' interval. He suggested that going by my medical history and general health condition, I should try out the two-week interval treatment. 'You will be able to withstand it,' he had said. Above everything, what appealed to me was that the ordeal would be over much earlier. In eight chemotherapy sessions almost two months would be saved. I decided to go for chemotherapy sessions at two-week intervals. If everything went well, the chemotherapy sessions would end on 30 January 2018.

During the surgery, a chemo port was inserted on the left side. This was to facilitate the administering of the chemotherapy drug. Otherwise the drug would have to be administered intravenously like usual drips, which becomes difficult and tiresome. The only drawback, apart from some additional cost, was that I had to carry this artificial object inside my body for the next two years after the surgery was over. The port had to be flushed before the main chemotherapy drug could be administered. The entire procedure of flushing the port and administering the drug usually takes about 4–5 hours.

My first chemotherapy session was on 24 October 2017. It was a Tuesday. I got up early, cooked breakfast. Chini had made a special request for an Iranian dish that I had learnt to cook from a TV show. She liked it a lot and I often cooked it for her. I thought, let me do it. Who knows how I will fare tomorrow after the chemo? Rice and dal had already been soaked the previous night. I quickly prepared the dish.

'*Kuchh kha lo,*' Mummy said.

'*Kha liya,*' I answered as I rushed to my vehicle. I left the house at 8.30 a.m. and was in office soon. My staff officer Mishra-ji was already there.

'Please files *le aiyye, kuchh kaam hai, main* 10.30 a.m. *tak nikal jaungi.* I will be back in the second half.'

He got all the pending work done without further questions. I continued with my work with a smile on my face as if nothing was wrong with me. I had to do it. My deep sense of self-respect and extreme scorn for sympathy kept me going. Moreover, I wanted to live with my head held high.

My Nana who stayed on and off with us in Sagar often used to say, 'Tough and distressful times prove the worth of a person. A strong person shines like gold in a prospector's pan while dealing with adverse circumstances.'

Devendra had managed to get leave to be with me for the chemotherapy session. He came to my office after some time. I got out of my office after finishing my work and walked to the standing vehicle in which Devendra was waiting. We left for the hospital. I had decided to be back in office after the chemotherapy session and complete the pending office work. We reached the hospital in about half an hour. As usual, the hospital atmosphere gave me cold feet. I felt as if I am watching a movie. I could barely fathom that the main character in the movie is me, Mridula–Ruby. The oncology ward of the hospital was too depressing. Seeing cancer patients battling various stages of the disease gave me a very uneasy feeling. The hospital administration and Dr Sahu heeded my request and arranged for the chemotherapy to be administered in the private ward.

Dr Sahu came and promptly started with the job. I was a bit anxious and my impatience showed, 'Please *zara jaldi karwa dijiyega,*' I said and followed it with my next question, '*Main kab tak* free *ho jaungi*?'

'Not to worry, Ma'am, *ho jayega,*' was his polite but terse reply.

After the routine check-ups like pulse rate and blood pressure, and the preliminary procedure of flushing the chemo port, the chemotherapy started. The drug started to flow through the chemo port and run in my blood, killing the disease. After some time, I realised that the flow of the drug through the drip pipes and the port was smoother at a particular angle. The flow would become very slow if I lay down or sat in different positions. I had to sit and could not lie down for the duration of the therapy. It all appeared boring, irksome and '*bakwaas*'. So I sat on my bed. Devendra had switched on the TV but who was interested in watching it? I was least interested in what was happening in the world. The romantic songs only brought back nostalgic memories when all was fine in our lives. Serials had never interested me. So I decided to make phone calls to some of my friends. Trying to be bold to everyone's, 'How are you?' I convincingly replied, 'I am very fine.'

I had recently been promoted as principal commissioner of Income Tax. Many congratulatory messages had come. I decided to reply to all. Finally the ordeal was over. I left the hospital with a pack of medicines for nausea, stomach problems, acidity, pain, etc. Infection of any type was to be avoided at all costs; the fever was to be promptly attended to. The WBC count was to be strictly monitored. By now I had memorised all the instructions.

Four injections of Grafeel were to be taken during the first week between two chemotherapy sessions. This was to boost my immunity and to maintain the WBC count. Blood tests were to be done in the following week before the next chemotherapy session scheduled for 7 November 2017.

On our way back from the hospital, I went to the office with Devendra and finished whatever work was to be done for the day. I met visitors in my office. Pretending to act as if 'all is OK' was a difficult task but not impossible.

Afterwards we decided to go to the mall. We went as if all was fine and it was a regular outing. We picked up dresses and cosmetics for Chini who was waiting at home. I had left early in the morning without meeting her. She was anxious to ask me about my day but kept quiet. I quickly ate some rice and rushed to my room. I hid my face in the pillow and cried. It was an awkward position to be in as, after my surgery, it had become difficult to lie on my side. I had to sleep on my back for several months after the surgery. I would lie keeping a pillow for support under my right arm.

The second day, post the chemotherapy, did not start on a good note. By morning, the drug had started taking effect. The nausea was extremely bad. Despite the heavy dose of antiemetics, I could not tolerate even a mouthful of water. Brushing my teeth and rinsing my mouth made me feel terrible. It reminded me of a pregnant lady's state. But I got ready and reached office, and continued with my work. Devendra came and sat with me. He tried to give me a lot of encouragement by saying, '*Ek ho gayi hai, dekhte dekhte poori* 8 *ho jayegi*'.

Chini was busy with her exams. Being my daughter, she has definitely inherited my traits of bravely taking on all the challenges that life throws at us. As a mother, I knew what all must have been on her mind. Despite my illness and the mental turmoil that she endured, she topped the university with 87 per cent marks.

As days passed, my condition became worse. Mummy was always by my side. She would caress my forehead and was ready to cook anything that I wished to eat. She often got custard or a paratha in the middle of the night but I could not eat even a morsel. I felt terrible even though I kept up a bold front. Devendra felt deeply saddened to see me lying on the bed, not even speaking a word. I had always been very chirpy and talkative. In the week after the chemo, my life was confined to office and my bedroom. I spoke to no one.

As the chemotherapy drug comes into effect, it kills the body's cancerous as well as normal cells. The body's immunity goes down and it is not in a position to fight any infection. Utmost care is to be taken to ensure that one does not catch any infection during chemotherapy. Two or three days after the chemotherapy are the most vulnerable. The highest standards of hygiene had to be maintained. Interaction with other persons was reduced to the barest minimum so that an infection was not passed on to me inadvertently. Only Devendra came to my room. No servant or maid was allowed. For those three or four days, Devendra only used to clean the room and bring anything to eat or drink if at all needed by me. Food would be cooked properly and eaten immediately to avoid any possible infection. I avoided eating salads, fruits, etc.

As the second week started, my condition improved slightly. Some energy and life started to flow in my limbs. I tried to speak, cook, talk and act normal. As Sunday would approach, precisely two days prior to the next chemo, I became edgy and upset. I always tried hard to hide it. Devendra encouraged me by saying something, '*Dekho, ab jaldi se* 30 January 2018 *aa jaye aur* chemotherapy *puri ho jayegi.*' Trying to save his leave for the future, he went back to his place of duty after two days.

As the days passed by, I put up a smile on my face and tried to be extra nice to all. My colleagues in office, congratulating me on my promotion, often asked when I would throw a party. I decided to organise a lunch for all my dear ones. Only two or three people in my office knew of my illness. They took special care to play host and made all the arrangements. Chini also attended and was a wonderful hostess.

It was my second chemotherapy, on 7 November 2017, and Devendra had arrived the same morning from Alwar. Realising that it will be difficult to balance his present official commitments as well as take care of the events unfolding on the family front, he had applied for a compassionate ground posting to Bhopal. His senior officers, Major General Sanjay Sharma and Brig. I.M. Lamba, strongly recommended his case and followed it up. Army headquarters took a very considerate view of his request. Some of his friends also helped. He was given an assurance that within a month's time he would be in Bhopal on a regular posting.

The day for the second chemotherapy session was also like the first one–rushing to the office early in the morning then to the hospital and back to office for work. The day was more tiring. I did not feel like going out anywhere; I just rushed back home from office and lay down on bed. Previously I had been a person who would never sleep in the afternoons; I would always get up in the morning, do my day's work and retire to my room only at night. But now lying in the room with my eyes closed was a new feeling altogether. I was totally unaware of what was happening around me.

Anyone speaking to me would elicit no response. Mummy or Chini would bring something to eat and I would continue to lie down. I had no strength to talk or respond. Mummy would try to feed me something with Devendra's help. I would eat a mouthful and then recline on the bed. I had no thoughts, no feelings and I could understand nothing. I just waited for time to pass, but it seemed to have come to a standstill.

In the initial years of my courtship when time stood still, it made me feel on top of the world. But now I felt nothing. In fact, at times, I did not even know where I was.

After the second chemotherapy, there was a new development–my hair started to fall. I knew it had to go, but when they actually went away, I broke down completely. By then I had taken on everything, the diagnosis, the numerous tests, the biopsy, the surgery, the aftermath of surgery, like carrying the drain on my body and also the chemo port and two chemotherapy sessions that had tested my patience and tolerance. But losing my hair... that was too much.

It took away everything–my spirit, my will, my courage and my self-confidence. Till now, I had tried to remain calm and composed but this devastated me completely. This is the worst thing that happened to me. Even the diagnosis of the deadly disease had not given me such sorrow and gloom. I did not know what to do. My hair started falling in huge clumps. My world had fallen apart. I spoke to Dr Sahu once it had started to fall and he replied, 'Madam, don't touch it or brush it. Let it just collect at the back of your head. That's how you will be able to keep it for a few more days.' In the office I started to cover my head with a scarf and pretended that I had a cold. This excuse was easily accepted.

I decided to talk to Dr Anurag Tiwari, 'My hair has started to go. In a day or two it will be gone completely. What do I do?' I almost wept.

'Don't worry, Ma'am, we will manage something.' His words comforted me but I wondered what he had in mind. Only a miracle could save me from the humiliation. In the evening I got a call from Dr Tiwari. He asked me to come to his clinic the next day.

I reached his clinic and got to know that a wig maker had been called. He came at around 12 p.m. Respecting my desire for secrecy and privacy, Dr Anurag did not disclose my identity.

After taking measurements, the man said, '*Ek hafta lagega*'.

I almost fainted, '*Nahin aap* please *jaldi kijiye. Ek hafta main to bahut* problem *ho jayega. Main utna* wait *nahi kar paoongi. Yeh mere bache khuche baal ek do dinn mein chale jayenge.*'

Dr Tiwari took him aside and spoke to him. Finally the man agreed to give it on Friday, which was four days away. But these four days felt like an eon. I kept quiet. Perhaps this was another test that I had to give. The repeated thought in my mind was, 'God, why me?' But I decided not to give up.

Dr Tiwari gave me a call on Wednesday morning, asking me to come to his clinic at 3 p.m. The '*wigwala*' had managed to weave new hair in just two days. Chini insisted on coming along. She had helped me so much when my hair started to bid me adieu. She used to carefully comb them, taking all the care to prolong the inevitable hair fall as much as possible. Chini cried when she cut the hair that had become a cluster behind my neck. I knew that a person who cries is the person who cares. So, on a Wednesday afternoon, in Dr Tiwari's personal quarters above his clinic, whatever was left of my hair was shaved off. It was traumatic. Nothing had upset me more. I wished I would cease to be. I cried hiding my face in the pillow behind closed doors.

I had also never been so upset in my life. My hair had been so pretty that it curled on its own very nicely at the ends. The hair dressers had always complimented me about my thick dark tresses. Now they were gone. The bald woman in the mirror was a stranger, not Mridula. I could not associate myself with her. My heart broke. It was someone totally different. I could not recognise myself. She did not look like Chini's mother. She did not even resemble the woman Devendra loved and cherished. How can anyone love or desire to be acquainted with such an obnoxious woman? It cannot be me. In deep anguish, there were no tears that I could shed for myself. But I realised that all this despair was only in me. I am fortunate to say that my family now loved me even more.

The wig maker fixed the new hair. It was a tricky job sticking them on. He told us about the precautions and maintenance of the hair weaves. Chini was of immense help. She had mastered the art of fixing it nicely and also maintaining it. Once fixed properly they appear pretty real and someone who was unaware would not be able to make out anything. This gave me a lot of confidence and increased my self-esteem tremendously. 'God! Why me?' I would keep asking myself. I had no answer. As a little girl I cried myself to sleep and crying does help a lot. I think sometimes tears speak more than words. Gloom can be the god of an unhappy person. I decided to hide my tears. So I tried to smile more. Although many a times I did realise that there was a need to cry and to be alone. Many a times I would say, 'Dear pillow, sorry for all the tears that I have given you.'

Perhaps there were many silent sufferers like me. There was disappointment at what else I may lose. Is it that easy to reject despair? I tried to console myself with small moments of happiness, little successes like being able to finish my day-to-day work in office despite my condition. I decided not to think of my failures or losses. I thanked God for all the nice people in my life. I thought of all my friends and family and acquaintances who were with me in this tough hour. I decided to dream of the future. I thought of a reason to live. I tried to overcome my dejection with hope. I knew happiness and hope kill misery. I recalled Edmond Dantès in the *Count of Monte Cristo:* 'The entire wisdom of this world is contained in these words, wait and hope.'

The Count of Monte Cristo has been one of my favourite books. Dr Harsh Mishra, my good friend and neighbour in Sagar, had narrated the story from an abridged version when I was a kid.

I always believed that there are no shortcuts in life. I had to live through these days. I kept my dreams alive and they in turn kept hope alive. I realised that life is nothing without hope.

In travelling through life's tough journey, I was lucky to have my sister Meenakshi's hand to hold. She had come for my third chemotherapy that was scheduled on 21 November 2017. Devendra could not come. He had got his posting to Bhopal and was busy winding up and handing over the charge in Alwar to his successor.

Dr Sahu was not there for the third chemotherapy, but all arrangements were in place. So we did not face any problems. Meenakshi had accompanied me to the hospital. During the chemotherapy, we kept chatting about old times. She likes to watch movies and had switched on the TV, catching up in between our talks.

Once the chemotherapy was over, I went to office for a short while and signed some important papers. On our way back home we did a lot of shopping, and bought books too. I pondered over life many a time. It pains me to confess that there are many who would be surprised and perhaps disappointed, if they were to learn about my illness and how I was able to come out of it due to God's blessings, the good wishes of my dear ones and Chini's prayers. It hurts. But it's OK, I have become used to all this. Life is like a wheel. It puts you down to lift you up. It moves you from despair to hope.

My friend, Dr Linki, told me to surgically remove such people out of my life as Dr Harit had surgically removed the disease out of my body. Linki, a very good friend, is a homoeopathic doctor.

In the next week, after the third chemotherapy, I started to have aches and spasms in my stomach. I came from office earlier than usual and spoke to

Dr Sahu. He advised to get my WBC count checked at once. The report showed the count at 1100. He advised that I get hospitalised immediately. I tried to argue with him, but he was adamant and I had to go to hospital. There was no one to go with me as my sister Meenakshi had already left. Mummy is too old and Chini was writing her semester examinations. I put up a brave front, packed some bare essentials in a carry bag and reached Dr Shrikant Jain's hospital.

He was kind enough and spared one of the nurses from his hospital, Sister Priyanka, who accompanied me. We went to the hospital in his car. I was hoping to be out of the hospital the next day, but I developed high fever the same night. Priyanka tended to me the whole night. She was the one who administered Avil and Paracetamol. She proved to be of immense help. She nursed and looked after me. She was the much-needed companion during those dark, long gloomy days, when I realised what it is to be alone. Even my surgery was not as upsetting as these three days in the hospital.

Priyanka and I would often talk. She was a light sleeper and would get up at night if I ever needed anything. The first night she did not sleep a wink.

Next morning, upon my insistence, she called the sister on duty to collect my blood sample to check the WBC count again. We hoped and prayed that the blood count may have increased by now. But to my shock, they had dropped drastically and were at about 600. We had to stay put in the hospital. More medicines had to be administered. Dr Sahu tried everything. He would frequently visit me to check my condition. Later, he told me that all the panic buttons were on when they saw such a low WBC count.

Priyanka kept my morale high by talking to me. We recited the *mahamantra*:

> *Hare Kṛṣṇa Hare Kṛṣṇa, Kṛṣṇa Kṛṣṇa Hare Hare,*
> *Hare Rāma Hare Rāma, Rāma Rāma Hare Hare.*
>
> हरे कृष्ण हरे कृष्ण कृष्ण कृष्ण हरे कृष्ण।
> हरे राम हरे राम राम राम हरे हरे।।

The WBC count increased on the third day, but they were somewhere around 1500 only. So I had to hang in there. By now I had become desperate to go home and told Dr Sahu, 'Doctor, I will run away. Please do something.' He just nodded. Priyanka and I had started praying again. By now I had been put on oral medicines. The next morning, Priyanka, on my insistence, again called the nurse on duty to collect the blood sample. Our prayers were finally answered and the counts increased to about 1800. This time Dr Sahu allowed me to go home.

By afternoon I was home. Mummy was there. Chini had gone to write her examination. I had a quick bath and rushed to office to catch up with my work and get going with my life as if nothing had happened. It was the end of November and a lot of work had piled up. For the three days that I was away from work, I wrote an application for casual leave. I made up a story that I was trying to exhaust my leave before the calendar year ended.

I am so grateful to Dr Abha and Dr Shrikant for holding my hand in times of crisis. They were with me from the very beginning.

The three days in hospital were a real eye-opener for me. I comprehended what loneliness can be. I remained upset for days remembering the hospital days. I am thankful to Sister Priyanka who did not know me at all but took care of me like a family member.

I thought of four of my novels published by Manjul Publications: *Jaane Kitne Rang Palash Ke, Aur Intezar Thak Gaya, Ab iss Dil Se Kya Kahun, Ek Khwaish Ne.* I read the reviews and remembered writing these books.

'जाने कितने रंग पलाश के', my first novel, had a beautiful review by Kamleshwar-ji, the renowned Hindi author. It was published in *आहा जिंदगी - कमलेश्वर की कलम से*:

मृदुला बाजपेयी के उपन्यास 'जाने कितने रंग पलाश के' में खास तौर पर प्रेमिल अनुभूतियाँ अभिव्यक्त हुई हैं। सैन्य जीवन मे प्रेम की भी कितनी अहमियत है, दुनिया जानती है। लेकिन जब प्रेम और देश सेवा के जज़्बे मे से किसी एक को चुनना होता है तो अक्सर प्रेम को ही बलि देनी पड़ती है। इस उपन्यास मे भी राष्ट्र प्रेम के जज़्बे को ऊपर रखा गया है। उभय संकट की ऐसी

स्थिति में पुरुष तो दो सीमाओं के युद्ध मे हर तरह के अरमान दबाये एकबार मे ही शहीद हो जाता है, लेकिन स्त्रियों को हर मोर्चे पर तिनका तिनका शहीद होना पड़ता है। ये उपन्यास स्त्रियों के इसी पक्ष को बड़ी खूबसूरती से उजागर करता है। जिसका पति या प्रेमी सीमा पर तैनात होता है, उसके दिल पर क्या गुजरती है, उपन्यास में इसे बखूबी व्यक्त किया गया है।

कथानक के अलावा इस उपन्यास को पढ़ने में इस की भाषा विशेष भूमिका अदा करती है। मृदुला बाजपेयी ने जो भाषा लिखी है, वह इस कथानक के प्रति उनकी संलग्नता को दर्शाती है।

उपन्यास में दो कहानियाँ एक साथ चलती हैं। एक का पहलू दुखद है, तो दूसरी का सुखद। दोनों पहलुओं को दिखने का आशय ये है कि यहाँ भी जीवन के दोनों रंग हाजिर हैं। जया और मृणालिनी के प्रेमी दोनों युद्ध मे जाते हैं, लेकिन जया का प्रेमी लौट नहीं पाता और मृणालिनी का प्रेमी वापस आ जाता है। इस तरह दोनों पहलुओं को दिखाकर लेखिका ने एक संतुलन बनाने की कोशिश की है। लेखिका का प्रयास निश्चित तौर पर प्रशंसनीय है कि सभी सैनिकों की पत्नियों या प्रेमिकाओं को निराशा का मुंह नहीं देखना पड़ता।

मृदुला ने एक नए विषय पर यह बहुत अच्छा उपन्यास लिखा है।

'और इंतजार थक गया' is the story of Damini Joseph, एक ऐसी लड़की, जो ढूँढने निकलती है अपने नाम मे छुपे हुये अर्थ को, अपनी पहचान और अपने अस्तित्व को, किन्तु जब सच्चाई उसके सामने आती है, तो उसे लगता है की उसका सब कुछ छिन गया है... और यहीं से दामिनी जोसेफ का नया जीवन प्रारम्भ होता है। जिसमे वह है, पूर्णता को तलाशता उसका प्यार है, और है उसके एकाकीपन की टीस लिए उसका सत्रह सालों से देवेंद्र

से मिलने का लंबा इंतजार...

It is a wonderful book. I recalled all the emotions that I had gone through while writing the book. It had a beautiful review by Imroz, the famous painter and partner of the great novelist Amrita Pritam. He had read the book and reviewed it on his own. I had not met him before. I happened to meet him subsequently in Delhi in 2010.

Another of my Hindi novels, 'अब इस दिल से क्या कहूँ' is a love story spanning two births. Its main protagonist is Anjali who suddenly develops special feelings for her new friend Shiva. The city of Prayagraj is like a character of the plot that witnesses the love blossoming between Anjali and Shiva.

I thought of all this and my spirits lifted.

Seven

The fourth chemotherapy session was on 5 December 2017. From here onwards the drug was supposed to be changed. Dr Sahu had said that the side effects of this new drug were not so severe. I was relieved.

The visit to the hospital in the intervening period had badly shaken me. I felt edgy and a strange fear gripped me at the very thought of the hospital. There was an apprehension of something unknown. I recalled what my friend Prasanna had said, 'Keep smiling because life is a beautiful thing and there is so much to smile about.' For, the smile hid my sorrow and pain. I tried to smile at everyone–the doctor, the nurse or anyone entering the room. I tried hard to be cheerful and talked to Devendra of our past–when we had walked in the snow in Dras, my shopping in the market of Kargil and our visit to Sela Pass to pay homage to my Mama, Captain Shukla. All this made me feel better and my world became a beautiful place.

Some of my doctor friends did help me a lot with their kind and encouraging words; they assured me that for the next four chemos, a different drug would be administered which would not reduce the blood count. As the day approached, I had reconciled myself to the fact that I had to go through with the chemo as there was no other alternative.

Devendra said, 'After today, you will be half way through.' This did help me for some time. But I was aware of my condition. Now I knew everything about chemotherapy–all the what, when and how of it. Still I was apprehensive. I consoled myself that at least half the ordeal will be over today. I tried to imagine that it was another normal day. I requested Dr Shrikant and he happily spared Sister Priyanka. So she accompanied me to the hospital.

The day passed and I had crossed half the bridge. This instilled fresh courage and optimism. At times I had been very unhappy and tried to teach myself not to expect more than life was willing to grant me. But now, since half the journey was over, it gave me confidence.

Meanwhile the chemo had started to affect in many other ways. I had barely overcome the shock of losing my hair and reconciled to putting on a wig when I realised that I was about to lose my nails. It was one harrowing experience after another. By the third chemo, all my nails had lost their sheen and begun to turn black. After a few more days, I realised that they had become lifeless and were getting uprooted. Sometime after the fourth chemo, one morning I woke up to a sharp pain on my thumb. I looked at my hands and shrieked. Devendra woke up, startled, and asked, '*Kya hua?*' Tears were rolling down my cheeks. I extended my hand towards him without saying a word. He was shocked to see my thumb. The entire nail was missing. It had fallen off somewhere. The pink flesh was visible. He looked around and saw the nail on the ground. It was as if someone had very neatly sliced it off with a surgical knife. Over the next few days, seven out of ten nails of my hands fell off, one by one. I had to keep the fingers bandaged to avoid any injury. The nails grew back after the chemo.

Another side effect of the chemotherapy were the blisters on my feet. After the third chemo, I could feel the skin being a bit sensitive. In a few more days, it appeared like I had walked on fire. There were big blisters. Slowly the skin began to peel off, bit by bit. I used to put on socks and keep the feet bandaged to avoid any injury. I was someone who always hated socks and never wore them. I often wondered, 'O God, what else is this illness going to make me do!'

The fifth chemo was on 19 December 2017. As I sat in the hospital with the new drug flowing through my body, I recalled so many happy memories from my childhood.

As a baby, I would often play under the jacaranda tree in full bloom and would pick up the scattered blue flowers from the ground with my small hands. On seeing my father, late Dr Sushil Kumar Bajpai, I would run to him and give him the lovely purple flowers. He always said that they looked very beautiful in my small hands. I would call out to him and he would pick me up in his arms. 'My delight, baby Ruby, a handful of purple sky is here in my arms.'

I would throw my arms around him, holding on to the purple blossoms. He would take the flowers and kiss my small hands.

I had spent so much time under the purple sky of the jacaranda trees. Every moment was a happy moment there. The essential duty of Premlal, the house boy, was to collect my toys, hair clips, story books, slippers, water bottle and numerous articles from the house and take them under the jacaranda tree where I would sit on the swing and spend my day.

I have a lot of fond memories of my father even though we had very little time together. I lost him when I was a little girl. He taught at the University of Sagar, and was a Ph.D. from Allahabad University, the Oxford of the East. He had been a propagator of education of the girl child. My sister and I went to the prestigious Saint Joseph's Convent Higher Secondary

School along with our elder brother, Priyadarshi Bajpai.

My father was a firm believer that a girl must be educated so that she is financially independent. We were groomed as individuals and not with the thought in our mind that '*Ladkiyo ko paraye ghar jana hai*'. He never considered us a burden. He taught his colleagues' daughters, who had opted for science as their subject and even other subjects, whenever there was a need. He helped several women who were studying as private students in the university with books and other things. My father's kindness knew no bounds. The newspaper vendor, Chaturvedi ji, was frequently offered a cup of tea. The vegetable vendor, who, because he left his house very early in the morning every day, could not carry his food, was offered something to eat whenever possible. The old *bade miyaan*, the *kabadi wala*, was treated with immense kindness and respect. *Bade miyaan* had fought as a soldier in Burma and had many stories to recount.

Father was a strict disciplinarian and our house had an atmosphere that encouraged studies. Many relatives and family friends stayed with us in Sagar and completed their studies from the university. Mummy took extra care of them. I am confident that they did not miss their homes and families during the years they spent with us in Sagar. My cousin, Anupam Bajpai, remembers his Sagar days as a golden period of his life.

My father taught me to value myself and made me realise my abilities to the fullest. He inculcated a strong sense of good values and, what I am today, I owe all of it to him. His care and protection have been a huge source of support and strength for me. He taught me so many things–the importance of honesty, extending a helping hand to others, caring for others, humility, kindness towards all, to name a few.

Once, as a little girl, when two of my front milk teeth had broken and an allergy of the skin had infected my legs up to my knees because of jumping in puddles caused after a day's heavy rainfall, I remember my father holding my little hand as we walked together. Whenever father went to the market, he always bought a toy or a book for me. He read out stories to me, he always thought I am the best. On my promotion as commissioner of Income Tax, I got posted to Allahabad, my ancestral place, and the place father had loved the most. I think, if he were alive, he would have been the happiest. In Allahabad I visited the university; it was a proud moment for me to see his name in the role of honours of the Ph.D. students. I had done him proud by joining the civil services and then serving at the Allahabad Income Tax Office. I think I am the best and my father's daughter. I lost my father suddenly in Jabalpur and it was the darkest day of my life.

The new year had arrived and I welcomed it in hospital while undergoing my sixth chemo on 2 January

2018. I don't know why in the hospital I became sad and pensive. I thought of all that I had lost in life—my father, my Nana and many of my friends. There is a pain in life beyond the physical. We all lose in life. But losing friends is agonising. I lost some of my friends to distance and some to time. I have kept their friendships in my heart and maybe some day I may get them back. I met some of my friends whom I had almost forgotten and, after forty years, I met an old friend. It was such a delightful experience. We relived all the happy moments spent together, going to the movies, eating in restaurants and playing cards.

Meanwhile, my friend and publisher Vikas suggested that I should work on my new book. Though I had started work on the fifth book, *Until You Come Home*, much earlier, I could not complete it due to my busy office schedule initially and my illness later. I liked the idea and started to finish the book which was due for publishing by Amaryllis. I shuffled through the manuscript and gathered my thoughts to continue from where I had left off.

Life had given me so much to remember. There was no need to feel sad. I grew up in Sagar, the most wonderful place on earth. Whenever I recollect places, memories of Sagar come rushing to me. I studied there and was very happy. It has been aptly said, 'Don't cry because it is over, rather, smile because it happened.' There is always a niggling feeling, a '*kaash*' that these days are gone. But their memories still fill me with joy.

My seventh chemotherapy was scheduled for 16 January 2018. The day was like any other. I was going through tough times. I had become used to it and decided not to get upset. When I would cry, Chini always hugged me, and then I cried some more. She often cried with me. The one who cries is the one who cares, I believe and can't reiterate enough. At times I had to try hard to hold back my tears but often I cried my heart out.

My eighth and final chemotherapy was scheduled for 30 January 2018. I had to take eight chemotherapy doses in all. I was happy that finally this ordeal was going to be over. I prayed that once this was over, I would never have to set foot in the hospital. These bouts of allergic reactions, skin ailments and taking dose after dose of Grafeel will all come to an end.

As I travelled with Devendra and Priyanka to the hospital, I recalled everything that had happened between 1 September 2017 and 30 January 2018. The diagnosis, biopsy, tests, surgery, wearing the drain on my body for nine days, the stitches being removed, the pain and after-effects of the chemos, all came to mind. The most traumatic thing was losing my hair. I could never reconcile to it even though I knew all along that it was imminent. I often asked Devendra, 'Why me?' Once, in utter despair I said, 'God, why not take me?'

'Thank God. You don't grant every wish,' he sighed.

Devendra loved me even when all my hair was gone. He had never seen me without hair as I always had the chemo cap on even when the wig was taken off.

We reached the hospital at the scheduled time. Dr Sahu was happy to see me smiling. After the routine check-ups and preparations, the medicines were administered. I was reminded of my days as a student at Sagar University. Life was so full of joy. Happiness had so many definitions then like wandering in the rain, strolling under the stars, a day full of smiles, bunking classes at times and much more. I recalled sitting with my friend Prasanna under a jacaranda tree in full bloom. Such delight it had given me. The fallen petals are a beautiful sight. Then we often wondered if the petals die and, who knows, go straight to heaven? Perhaps they did. We would often pick them up and wish for so many things. Prasanna said that anything wished would be granted because the petals would take the wish to heaven. Prasanna, where are you, dear? You made me laugh when at times I felt like crying. I lost her to time. Prasanna, I miss you and will always remember you.

When I went to Sagar after my treatment was over, I realised walking alone is not at all difficult but coming back alone is quite tough. Here I had walked together with a friend. I felt tears prick my eyes and I cried.

I relived writing my book *Ek Khwahish Ne*–'एक ख्वाहिश ने'. The beautiful words on the back flap of the book came back to haunt me.

'कुछ ख्वाब इतने खूबसूरत होते हैं की टूट जाने के बाद भी आँखें बंद रखने का मन करता है। जिंदगी हाथ से कहाँ फिसलती जाती है? मुट्ठी छोटी ही सही लेकिन अगर कसकर थाम लो तो मुट्ठीभर जिंदगी तो अपनी हो ही जाएगी। आज शायद मुट्ठीभर जिंदगी भी कहाँ बची थी मेरे पास।'

I thought of the book.

हिबा, तारा और आकाश की जिंदगी को बयान करते पन्ने उन रिश्तो की जबान बने हैं जो जीवन के उतार चढ़ाव और अस्थिरता की सच्चाई को सामने लाते हैं। इसे समय का चक्र कहें या इंसान की मजबूरी या फिर नियति का लेखा, कुछ घटनाएँ और निर्णय जिंदगी को इस कदर प्रभावित करते हैं की किसी का आज बीते हुये कल की आग से झुलस जाता है। कुछ ऐसा ही हुआ तारा के साथ, और क्या हिबा इससे अनछुई रह पाई? क्या आकाश इन दुश्वारियों के लिए वाकई जिम्मेदार था? क्या तारा उसे माफ कर पाई?

Tears rolled down my eyes thinking about them. On my way back, I was happy that I had finally taken the chemos. I felt like singing. I told Devendra to play some songs on the car's music system. And the song that came by chance was one of my favourites–'*Aaj main upar, aasman neeche...*' Chini as a small child had often danced to this number.

It was a big relief now. There was going to be no nausea, no stomach upsets, no low WBC count. The constant fear that something might go wrong was going to go away.

Eight

By now I had successfully crossed the second stage of the treatment. This was to be followed by twenty-five sessions of radiotherapy which would take about forty-five days as the sessions were from Monday to Friday. The doctor told me that each radiotherapy session was going to take about half an hour. It had indeed been a long bridge that I had to cross. Though I had covered some distance, a lot was still left. I was just halfway across the bridge. But the fear of a fast-flowing stream below and the oscillating bridge did not haunt me anymore. I was midway and I knew that I could easily be on the other side.

Before the radiotherapy another PET scan was to be conducted. To go through that process all over again was frightening and it upset me initially. I reminded myself that I had undergone this PET scan before and there was nothing to be afraid of. Finally the scan and some other routine tests were done. Everything was fine and the radiotherapy was started.

As I wanted to avoid running into any known faces, it was decided that the technicians who would be doing it would give me a ring as soon as the last person was in. I would then reach there in time. The two female technicians administering it were angels. They were very sensitive to my need for privacy and secrecy.

Everything was going fine. In between, I had to go to Vidisha for some official work. The trip went well. This was the first time that I had moved out of Bhopal since October 2017. Devendra and Chini insisted that I must go. They were eagerly waiting for me. 'How was the day?' Chini asked enthusiastically. 'I am so happy that you could make it,' Devendra added.

'Everything was fine but for the food. I could barely swallow some rice and finish two big bottles of Bisleri,' I replied.

The days progressed normally and the radiotherapy went fine for the initial two weeks. But by the third week I developed swelling in my throat. I was unable to gulp even water. My appetite went down. I could barely eat two spoons of rice. Swallowing anything, even semi solids or liquids, became difficult. Pain killers did not help. The radiotherapy started to affect me. My skin turned red and then black. By the twelfth day it had cracked and was full of blisters. The therapy had to be stopped in between for a week, although I had become used to my Monday to Friday radiotherapy sessions.

The break gave me a chance to devote more time to the departmental in-house magazine that I was tasked with to edit. Mr P.K. Dash had joined as our new principal chief commissioner. A very dynamic person, he was full of innovative ideas. Once he came to know that I had four published books to my credit, he entrusted me with the task of editing the in-house departmental magazine. He would assign responsibilities to me, and sometimes even a bit more than any other officer of my seniority. The magazine was a success and it was launched with a lot of fanfare. Another extracurricular activity that he entrusted me with was to organise a run for spreading tax awareness–'Taxathon'–on the occasion of Income Tax Day in July 2018. Devendra also helped me with his meagre NCC staff and cadets. This again was a very successful event widely covered by the media and much appreciated by Mr Dash. All these events were over and above my mandated task of tax collection. By now I had been posted as principal commissioner of Income Tax, Bhopal. I had a huge target of collecting a few hundred crores. It was a seemingly unachievable target, much more than the previous year. But I set about achieving it. I took it as a challenge. I had to really push myself to ensure that my targets were achieved. Not only did I achieve my target, I also exceeded it. When Mr Dash had joined in November 2017, just after my first chemotherapy, I did not tell him about my illness and the treatment that I was going through. I went about my business as usual, never expecting any sympathy because of my illness. He was kind enough to sanction my occasional casual leaves that I used to request in the course of the treatment. He ultimately came to know after a few months when I forwarded my application to be permitted to stay back in Bhopal. He called me immediately after seeing my application. 'Why didn't you tell me?' he demanded. He was shocked.

'I shall never forgive you. I am feeling bad that I kept on burdening you with additional tasks. Had I known, I would have never done it. And hats off to you, Mridula, you took on everything without ever complaining,' he added apologetically.

'Sir, please, you have been so kind to me. I never wanted to be seen as playing the victim and seeking sympathy. Taking on every task as if I have no illness has made me stronger. It has probably speeded up my recovery,' I said.

Mr Dash was very nice and considerate. He signed my application, strongly recommending my retention. He assured me that he would also put in a word to explain the genuineness of my case.

Many times I sat alone and wished that the

radiotherapy sessions would resume and wished for all this to end. By now the trees had shed most of their leaves. As a child I had loved walking on the fallen leaves. The sound of my feet on the leaves was still as musical as ever. Autumn had been my favourite season. Somewhere I had read that God seemed to have put one season that was autumn just for the beauty of it. I have always loved February. February sunsets are lovely. The fallen leaves would cover the path so beautifully. I recalled my old days in Sagar and my spirits soared. The time from September 2017 to January 2018 had been tough, painful and difficult, but all those days were over and had almost come to an end now. There was no pain, only a feeling of the pain that once was.

Soon March and April would arrive. The roadsides would be full of jacaranda blooms, along with those of Gul Mohar, Palash and Amaltas, each more beautiful than the other. But the jacaranda blooms brought a different kind of joy. It brought back so many haunting memories. By the time radiotherapy would be over, the jacaranda would be in full bloom, in a way symbolizing that I have fully recovered.

The skin on my body had turned as black as coal. My mother happened to see my back one day and wept. The lotions and creams did help and gradually the broken skin healed. The skin in that area is dark even to this day. I have a huge scar too. Time heals all wounds, it is rightly said. With time I have learnt so many new things. I learnt to respect and love my scars. The scars and the bruises are the medals that one earns as one learns a lot from them. The scars show that you have been through a battle in life and have emerged stronger and triumphant. Initially, I was scared to look into the mirror. But now, not only do I look into a mirror, I also do not react when I see my scars. I have learnt to accept and even love them. These scars are nothing as compared to the scars human beings leave on a person's soul. The scars will be there for a long time, maybe for a lifetime, but they are a sign that the wound has healed, the illness is cured. I could cross this endless sea of tough times by slowly living through each day, each surgery, each physiotherapy, each chemo, each radio, the medicines and, above all, maintaining a positive attitude and accepting these tough times as part of God's test.

My positive bent of mind helped me and I never gave up. I could be successful in my endeavour. This was easy as the people around me were happy, warm and genuine. I realised that optimism and faith in God kept me going through my illness. Always choose hope as I had read and hope gave me confidence in myself. Many times I had to make my own hope. I hoped for a better tomorrow and am sure that it will turn out to be better than what I can imagine. This world is an echo. What you give to the world comes back to you. So give love, be kind to all, help the needy, pray for all. Listen to your heart. What is meant for me will always be there and what I miss was really never meant for me.

Nine

Once three stages of treatment–surgery, chemotherapy and radiotherapy–were over, we decided to visit Allahabad. Chini was very happy that my treatment had gone as per schedule, with very little complications.

Since my surgery, this was the first long journey by train that I was undertaking. Devendra and I have great faith in the Hanuman temple, opposite the High Court in Allahabad. We have been regular visitors to the temple for years. During my posting at Allahabad, I visited the temple regularly every Tuesday and Saturday.

The visit brought back fond memories. Allahabad has been very special to all of us as my father studied here, my mother came here as a young bride of sixteen. I spent happy times with Devendra when he was posted here. Chini loves the place for all the restaurants–El

Chico, Tamarind Tree, Hotel Kanha Shyam and, of course, Sangam, where the three rivers meet. She visited all these places and was very happy. The visit to A.H. Wheeler bookshop in Civil Lines brought back old memories when I had taken Chini as a child and bought books of fairy-tales and comics for her. We relived those happy days when stories from these books were read out to her. She loves to listen to fairy-tales.

I recall the helping attitude of my paternal grandfather, Pandit Lakshmi Narayan Bajpai. He had a small family of six people, but took care of our extended family and many of our relatives. As Allahabad was the hub of education with several examinations being held there, along with continuous litigations going on at the High Court, there were at least 40–50 people staying in our house at any given time. The city is also known for its pilgrimage sights, most importantly the Sangam. So it was a busy household the entire year. My grandfather is still remembered by all as an extremely generous and kind person. He took care of the children of his relatives as if they were his own. Maybe I could sail through my illness because of the good deeds he had done without expecting anything in return.

In the morning we did puja at the Hanuman temple and sought the blessings of the Lord Almighty. We offered clothes to the deity and a flag was put on the terrace of the temple. We lit diyas under the peepal tree. I have mentioned the lighting of diyas in my novel, *Until You Come Home.*

After a wonderful but short visit, we got back. I continued with my medicines and exercise. The three-monthly check-ups were to follow and the monthly flushing of the chemo port was a must. Life slowly started getting back to normal. Many a times I felt as if all that happened was a bad dream. But when I looked at myself in the mirror or removed my wig, the person I saw was a changed version of myself.

A number of doctor friends became my lifeline during these eight months. Friends like Dr Shrikant Jain and Dr Subodh Varshney proved to be pillars of support since the initial days when the illness was diagnosed.

Dr Shrikant Jain and Dr Abha Jain, my long-time friends, were the first to learn of my illness. Both of them were very supportive and kind. They gave instances of medical history where innumerable persons in a similar or possibly a much worse condition had overcome their illness successfully and lived a healthy life for 25–30 years post-treatment. This greatly boosted my spirit and morale. Such things being told by my doctor friends immensely motivated me to move ahead. It's true that life cannot be predicted. If people could predict what lies ahead, life would cease to be what it is. The journey of life has been difficult during these past eight months, but now I seemed to understand it better. I realised that through kindness for others, having a helpful attitude is important. But being in love with one's own self is a great motivator. Once you are in love with yourself everything falls in place. In September 2017, when I was diagnosed with the illness, Dr Shrikant told Chini, '*Dekhna* Diwali *tak aapki* Mummy *achhi ho jayengi*'. My sweet Chini was greatly reassured although I thought that when Dussehra itself was so distant, who could think of Diwali? But I had to be brave.

Abha and Shrikant regularly visited my family during the intervening period of my diagnosis and my frequent visits to Delhi that followed and took care of my family. Their help cannot be measured and quantified. It was infinite and perhaps much beyond that.

Dr Harit Chaturvedi is one of the most positive, nice and sweet persons that I have ever met. Despite dealing day in and day out with this deadly disease, he remains full of positivity and his healing touch is divine. He infuses his patients with the much-needed hope.

He performed the surgery and even came to see me in my room at 11 p.m. He sounded confident of my quick and speedy recovery and said that I would be discharged from the hospital the very next day. He had done the surgery and he knew about it in detail. He assured Devendra that I would do fine and there was no cause for any concern. Dr Harit's contribution in my recovery is immense. He gave me his time and was always available to respond to the innumerable queries I had. It was because of his fine surgery that I was able to leave the hospital in 24 hours and there were no complications later. Everyone was surprised that I had left the hospital after 24 hours of surgery. I owe my second lease of life to Dr Harit Chaturvedi.

Dr T.P. Sahu, my medical oncologist, did all the eight chemos. He saved my life. After the second chemo, my WBC went down as low as 618. The situation appeared scary but his magnificent combination of care and professionalism made the tough times end soon. His experience and skill in dealing with my illness always appeared to be godsend. He held my hand during those days. He gave me hope and that made those days appear less difficult. Despite his busy schedule he was always available and extended his help at all times. When I went to meet him, initially, I had been a bit apprehensive. He has the reputation of being curt and impatient. But I beg to differ. He answered all the questions that I posed with patience. He even did jobs like setting the needle in the chemo port when the nurses could not do it. During the chemo sessions, at the slightest problem, he would rush to my room and promptly attend to the problem. He knew his responsibility and did a great job. My illness stood no chance before the competence of Dr Sahu. During the chemo sessions we would also have a friendly chat regarding general issues.

It was his care and experience that I could go through eight chemotherapy sessions on a fifteen-day interval, which is a tough call. My heartfelt gratitude to him and my countless thanks to God that I could find a doctor like him. He came as a magician and gave me new life. I wish him happiness and long life. May all good things come to him.

Dr Subodh Varshney needs special mention. He had explained in detail about the surgery, chemotherapy, radiotherapy and what was to be the line of follow-up treatment.

'Madam, don't worry. Your diagnosis has been very timely. It's not at all late,' he had told me when I met him immediately after my biopsy.

'What chances do I have of...' I could not even bring myself to complete the sentence.

'Oh! It is going to be cured 200 per cent and you are going to be alright,' was his spontaneous reply.

'But it's a deadly thing and why me?' I had asked him.

'Madam, it's the most curable form of this disease. This form has the highest rate of survival. No need to be scared. Nothing will happen. I will soon see you having tea with me and discussing the latest movie,' he reassured me with a soothing smile.

Dr Subodh gave me the much-needed encouragement

and confidence that my condition was not bad. He motivated and assured me that I will soon be fine. I was now confident that I am going to be a survivor; to put it more appropriately, I am one. Had it not been for him, I would have succumbed to depression and despair, or I may not have been able to put up a fight. He gave me the will, the confidence and moral support to deal with it.

Dr Anurag Tiwari and his wife Aparna played an important role during my illness. Anurag and Aparna were very caring and respected my desire for secrecy about the whole thing. Nobody got even a whiff of it. They helped a lot to get my new set of hair. Having the hair back restored my confidence and my self-esteem greatly. I cannot find words in any dictionary to thank them. Aparna, my friend of so many years, did all she could to console me.

I feel deep gratitude when I recall even now, how Aparna painted my nails to hide their black colour. The countless Band Aids she put on my nails to protect the tender skin. She was a pillar of support. A friend and a doctor's wife, she spoke kind and comforting words. She always spoke of women who were survivors of this deadly disease. Anurag and Aparna were very sensitive to my need for privacy and did not disclose my condition to anyone. I continued to visit them for treatment on account of various complications and side effects which were always very promptly dealt with. I also went and sat with them whenever I needed rest as they were close to my office.

I met Dr Sunil Kumar after my radiotherapy. He was to be my oncologist for the follow-up three-monthly regular check-ups. I met him for the first time in June 2018 with my blood test reports. He was very considerate and caring. He answered all my questions. He convinced me that the illness was over and there was nothing to worry. He always encouraged me to keep my morale high. He was available for any consultation. His biggest quality is his positive approach and every patient is very special to him. He creates a certain comfort level with all his patients. He said healing takes time. He was willing to hear me and speaking to him helped immensely. Dr Sunil Kumar was able to bring out my calm side. Earlier, I would try to remain calm but there was always a feeling of restlessness and anxiety. He laid emphasis on a positive attitude and how it is important to lead a stress-free life. He came in my life to heal me. His better half, Dr Krishna, who is a dentist, became a very good friend. We discussed so many things together from astrology to movies. She is one of the kindest souls I have come across. On many occasions, when I developed fever or fell sick, Dr Sunil and Dr Krishna were the first ones to come to my house to look me up.

Many came forward to support and extend help. A special mention here would be of Gaurav Sharma and Saurabh Sharma, our long-time neighbours. Saurabh visited me every morning and every evening when I was hospitalised with low WBC. He religiously accompanied us for my fourth, fifth, sixth and seventh chemotherapy sessions.

He was there at the hospital when I was there to flush the chemo port which was to be done every month. Gaurav extended his support by sending my representation to Delhi for my retention at Bhopal. Both are my good-luck charms.

I have no words to thank Col N.S. Bevli, the then commanding officer of my husband's parent regiment and his successor, for his unstinted support throughout this period. He extended all the support that we needed during and after my surgery.

Sister Priyanka accompanied me to the hospital and was with me for four days when I was admitted between the second and third chemotherapy sessions. My friends, Dr Abha and Dr Shrikant, had sent Priyanka to be with me. Priyanka was not only efficient in nursing but she took care of me during those dark days when there was no one with me. My aged mother could not have gone and Chini had her exams. Priyanka tended to me, prayed with me, gave me my medicines on time and did not make me miss any family member. Her care, affection and devotion made me feel blessed.

During my treatment, Sanjay, the buddy of my

husband, took care of us in so many ways. His devotion to us and respect for my mother, Chini and me is out of this world. Depen Tamang, the other buddy, looked after me at the time of my surgery. He came when Sanjay was on leave. He even emptied the drain attached to my body, gave me my medicines regularly and on time and helped me with my arm exercises. No questions asked, never a grudge for having to do something extra. It's very unfortunate that we lost him in a tragic accident in March 2019 when he was in the field area. Any soldier committed to a task does it with a high sense of devotion to duty and loyalty. I will always remember their selfless devotion. Both of them were very simple, honest and good.

All my friends helped in one way or the other. I am fortunate to have such friends. They were there for me in my good times like my book launches, my promotions, the celebration on Chini's excellent academic performance, Devendra's regiment receiving a citation, him getting commendations, etc. They were also there in the rough moments of my illness and the times in between. Each one of them did a world of good for me.

My best friend always said that if I live to be hundred, he would want to live a day less so that he would never have to live without me. But I lost him in the hustle and bustle of life. May he be happy and have all the blessings of God.

Anjali Tripathi is a dear friend and I thank God every day for giving me a friend like her. She got me an appointment with Dr Harit Chaturvedi, the Oncologist (surgeon) in Delhi. She spared her precious moments and was always available for any help. Even before I landed in Delhi for a detailed check-up prior to the surgery, she had fixed everything with Dr Harit. Times were tough but all help and support made things easier. She spoke to Dr Harit whenever any consultation was needed. She is the kindest person who has regularly kept in touch from the time of diagnosis to this day. She spoke encouraging words to my mother and daughter when I had gone to Delhi for surgery. I thank her sincerely for everything she did. When a year had passed since the diagnosis, she rejoiced with me.

As the days pass, I think that in life, to find a special friend who makes life special by just being there is rare. Anjali is that friend. Whenever I felt low, she convinced me that there was a door of hope waiting to be unlocked. Anjali, I have so many friends but you will always be irreplaceable and special. Someone has rightly said, 'We don't meet people by accident, they are meant to cross our paths for a reason. It's rare to find people who take you from the dark places and lead you back to light.'

Dr Linki Agarwal turned out to be another great friend. I owe a lot to her for it was she who not only cajoled me but rather pushed me to go and get all my tests done in September 2017. She is a good homeopath and I consulted her regarding the lumps in my breast. She refused to give any consultation but told me to go to a doctor immediately for the ultrasound and mammography. She had said very sternly, 'If there is no pain and the lumps have been there for some time, it's rather serious.' And the next day I was getting my USG, mammography and biopsy done. Thanks, Linki, else I may have postponed it to another day and would have lost out on valuable time.

When I met Dr Harit he said, 'You are just in time. Not too late, not too early.' The disease could have spread further. Linki, you played a crucial role in this second lease of life for me.

My real support came from my family. During my illness I realised that the most important thing I have is family. The feeling that they are there for me made me sail through those threatening dark days. They all came forward–Mummy, Devendra, Chini and Meenakshi. They put up with my mood swings and emotional outbursts. At times, I was really very horrible to them. They put up with all this and did everything ungrudgingly. I also learnt that family is not always blood relations but all the people around us who are there with you.

A sister is worth a thousand friends. My sister Meenakshi would ring up every day. On the days of my chemo she wished me luck very religiously. She came so many times to see me. She went to Alwar to get our stuff packed when Devendra was posted on compassionate ground to Bhopal. I can recall countless small things and how they all took care and made me feel so loved. I am very fortunate to have a family that is always there with me. They held my hand always. My mother, my sister, my husband and my daughter make up my family. I realise that family is the most important thing in the world. My loving family is the God's greatest gift to me. They were so caring, so supportive and did countless things for me. They provided me with strength and security. This feeling was very important to enable me to come out of my illness. The love they showered in turn gave me immense strength. I wish to celebrate them and the major role they played in my recovery. My small and close-knit family made me realise who I could turn to when times were tough.

I say to all, always love your family. Family teaches us to do so much for one another and expect no returns, no exchanges. In life, it is important to have a family. I feel sorry that I was unkind to them at times during my illness. Mummy was with me throughout the period of my illness. She has always been my backbone. Mummy, who is in her eighties, would be at my side massaging my hands and feet as I had started to have terrible pain in my limbs after the chemotherapy sessions. Her strength has always in turn given me strength. She has been through a lot–she lost her mother when she was very young, she lost her only brother, Captain K.L. Shukla, in the war of 1962 and her husband early on in life. I am a survivor today because of her blessings and it was her prayers that helped me endure everything. She constantly prayed. She had done a lot of good to many. A number of relatives studied at Sagar University where my father, Dr Sushil Kumar Bajpai, taught in the department of Botany. Mummy had looked after them. It was her good karma that came in the form of my second life. She is my mother and my everything. I am often reminded of the famous quote by Khalil Gibran, 'Mother, the most beautiful word on the lips of mankind.'

My husband, Brigadier Devendra Pandey, an army officer, did his duty and immediately applied for a compassionate ground posting to Bhopal. He left Alwar where he was serving in an important assignment. We tried and he got posted here before my third chemo started. He got an extended joining time too. Devendra was posted in a NCC Battalion responsible for training students. It must have greatly affected his future career prospects. He spent so much on my treatment, was always by my side, he tolerated my mood swings, comforted Chini who needed support, tried to do work that he had never done before like cooking, cleaning even washing dishes at times. Devendra, who did not even know how to light the gas burner or switch on the induction, became a good cook. He made tea for me or made oats, custard or porridge once in a while. I did not feel like eating at all. He would always cajole me to eat, '*Kha kar to dekho kaisa bana hai?*'

'*Maine try kiya hai*,' I would get irritated and tell him. 'I am nearly finished *aur tumko khane ki padhi hai?*'

After uttering these words I would immediately realise that he said all this so that I may eat something. Thus, I ended up eating a little. The blisters in my mouth and nausea had taken away all my appetite. I generally survived on a small bowl of custard. In the days that followed the chemo, I could barely eat half a roti or paratha.

He massaged my aching hands and feet, kept awake with me, escorted me to my office. His strength reminded me of Tarzan or Phantom the way he faced all the challenges. Devendra, I am lucky to have you as my life partner. I go back to those days when we had first met. I often remember those days that cheered me up during the painful ones of my illness. The grass under our feet is still green, there is bright sunshine around us and there is blue sky above us. I am confident that whenever there is rain, there will be a rainbow soon after. It was your love that gave me the courage to put up a brave fight. Devendra, you mean so much to me that I cannot imagine life without you. I read this quote in school, but realized its true meaning only now.

'Love is not a single act, but a climate in which we live, a lifetime venture in which we are always learning, discovering, growing. It is not destroyed by a single failure or won by a single caress. But love me for love's sake.'–Ardis Whitman

Chini is the centre of my world. My world revolves around her. She is the most precious person in my life. I am the closest to her and I came out of this illness only because I had to live for her. It's very aptly said, 'Daughters are born mothers.' She stood by me in my bad times and gave me hope when I had almost surrendered to despair. Chini often used to be up at midnight, rushing to cook custard for me or would ask me if I needed a cup of tea. She always likes to get up late in the morning but as I had to leave early and on the day of the chemo much earlier, she would wake up earlier than her usual time. Every day she very dutifully fixed my artificial hair. She washed and dried them. When the wig started to lose its shine, she tried each and every shampoo one could think of to make them appear good. She with her untiring efforts maintained my artificial hair for almost a year. She painted my nails with bright colours, started to put on matching eyeliner and danglers to make me look good. This greatly restored my self-confidence.

When the hair on my eyebrows fell, she made them with a pencil. She did a fantastic job and they looked real and natural. Next when my eyelashes fell, she applied eyeliner. I was reminded of those days when she was a baby and I used to dress her up, and I felt very proud to be the mother of such a pretty child. Now she was decking up her mother but in what terrible circumstances. She had turned into a mother for me. She always ensured that I put on new and nice clothes. I had changed my appearance totally so that no one would notice the real change. Earlier I had never painted my nails, had never worn earrings or applied eyeliner. I had gone to office with a bindi on my forehead and a light shade of lipstick, that was all. Chini had so much conviction in my strong will power that I would survive, that's why here I am the survivor. She asked me to focus on my new book, *Until You Come Home*, and would always ask me, '*Kitne* page *ka* correction *kiya*?' I corrected the draft of my book during the long, boring and arduous chemo sessions.

Chini tried hard and rarely wept or cried before me and whenever I would break down, she would hug and console me. She very generously complimented me on my good looks which, in reality, had totally vanished. I knew she was speaking from her heart and it was her love for me that made her see beauty and appreciate my looks when I had turned so ugly–no hair, no nails, no eyebrows, no eyelashes.

Slowly my eyebrows started to appear and gradually my eyelashes came back. Chini massaged my head with Mintop oil religiously and would always speak encouragingly, '*Abhi to thode din mein chota juttu ban jayega*,' even when my hair showed no signs of any growth. She showed a lot of understanding and maturity and took my mood swings in her stride.

The ever-demanding little girl had grown into a mature lady. She empathised the maximum. On one occasion she broke down before me and said, 'Mamma you help so many people, you are good to all, why did it have to be you?'

I had no answer and the two of us wept. In October 2018, almost after one year, Chini said while fixing my hair, 'Now you will not go to office with this artificial hair. The short hair looks so nice and you look much younger. We can pass of as sisters instead of mother and daughter.' She and Devendra then prevailed upon me and I went to office with short hair.

Devendra accompanied me. Every one was stunned at my new hairstyle. Few ladies even appreciated it. But for Chini, I would have continued with my artificial hair much longer. Next day Chini gave the hair to a hospital to be used by some needy person. She wanted to get rid of all such things as soon as possible as they were a reminder of those dark days.

I am in the civil services because of the keen efforts of my massi, Mrs Malti Mishra. She had come to Sagar from Lucknow when the advertisement for filling up the form for the preliminary examination appeared in *Employment News*. She cut it, filled it up and went to the post office to buy the postal order. I merely signed the form. My centre for prelims was Lucknow. I stayed with her where she looked after me. Her affection for us cannot be measured. My cousin Alok Mishra, commonly referred to as 'Bhai-ji', dropped me at the centre for the civil services preliminary examinations. He also brought me lunch during the break.

I lost my dear massi during the pandemic. She was old but we all wanted her to be there. We had spent nine long years together in Lucknow, when I was posted there. A regular visitor to our house, she had been with us through our ups and downs. Every weekend when we were in Lucknow, we spent in her house. My massi very often cooked *poori aloo* for us and it was the tastiest *poori aloo* I have ever eaten.

I feel extremely sad that I could not visit Lucknow after she passed away. Mummy was totally shattered and heart-broken at the loss of her dear elder sister. She was inconsolable in Bhopal and Meenakshi had to take her to Mathura. Chini and I have always lived with Mummy and we are used to having her around. Her sudden departure totally devastated us. I can only say that Covid-19 times have been really tough for all and specially for me on a personal account.

Chini is very fond of her Alok Mama and Madhu Mami. Bhai-ji is an excellent human being. Anyone in need of anything can knock on his door even at 2 a.m. He is spiritually inclined and a very disciplined person.

In my workplace when anyone has ever a word of praise for me or says a good word about me, I always tell that I owe it to my mentor and senior K.D. Gupta, an IRS Officer of the 1966 batch. He taught me so much, not only about IT, but also how to deal with other matters. Only technical skills do not run the office, a good officer has to be a combination of so many qualities. I am yet to see a more humane, considerate and caring person who has walked the face of this earth. He was full of empathy for all. The years spent under him were the best years of my career. Recently I met him after a long time, and the message that he sent after returning to Kanpur was, 'I am so happy to see you happy.' God seldom creates such people. I'm fortunate to have known him. He always said, 'Let's do it' and never said, 'You go and do it.' I have had the good fortune of knowing him since my training days as a probationer at the National Academy of Direct Taxes, Nagpur, our Alma Mater. I was fortunate enough to serve under him again at Lucknow when he was the commissioner and subsequently chief commissioner.

Another person I often remember is Dr Rajiv Dube, whom I used to tie rakhi. He was much elder to me but we did our ad hoc lectureship at Sagar University together. He invariably dropped me to the university. I taught English to B.Pharmacy students where he was also teaching. At times we would sit on the terrace and talk about movies, novels, spirituality, etc. He introduced me to the world of Hindi literature. He gave me books like *Pratham Pratishruti*, *Sahib Biwi aur Ghulam*, etc., to read. We also talked of English books like *The Far Pavilions*, *Jewel in the Crown*, *To Kill a Mockingbird*, *The Fountainhead* and many more. It's deeply saddening that we lost him in 2009. I had read a quote long ago, which says, 'Sharing tales of those we have lost is how we keep away from really losing them.'

Rajiv Bhai Sahab was a pillar of support when I lost my Nana in 1982. I was greatly disturbed. I had a lot of stress and would be upset. Losing Nana was the greatest tragedy of my life and I did not know how to deal with it. Bhai Sahab was my counsellor and friend in those days.

A person who played a great role in my life and my grooming was Dr G.S. Tripathi, a dear friend of my father. He taught history at Dr Hari Singh Gaur Vishwavidyalaya, Sagar. I address him as Chacha-ji. His affection and care towards my family knew no bounds. After my father's death, we were contemplating whether to shift to Lucknow. Chacha-ji handed over the keys of his ancestral house in Lucknow to us, so that we could live there as long as we wanted. His house was in Arya Nagar, close to my massi-nani's house. However, we continued to stay in Sagar. But his gesture touched us. He always rose to the occasion as a true friend of my father. He gave me a Parker pen when I was selected for the civil services. I joined my service in January 1989, using the same pen to fill up various forms.

Come December and I lost one of my dearest friends, Reeta Singh, affectionately called Ritu. It's a great personal loss for me. I did not even know that she had passed away. I decided to call her one day. Her daughter answered the call and broke the sad news. There are so many things all around to remind me of the lovely times we had in Lucknow, the regular visits to coffees shops and the frequent shopping sprees. These fond and cherished memories will hold her in my heart forever. She was a great soul. Her memories will always remain with me.

Ten

My colleague and friend Neeraja Pradhan held my hand from the beginning till the end. It has been very rightly said, 'A friend in need is a friend indeed.' Right from the moment of the diagnosis to surgery and throughout the chemotherapy, radiotherapy and afterwards she showed utmost care. She spoke words of encouragement and her behaviour displayed tons and tons of affection which was the need of the hour.

Neeraja's letter that I was suffering from malignancy and was posted at Bhopal, undergoing treatment after surgery at the local hospital, helped immensely in getting my husband posted to Bhopal on compassionate ground. She respected my wish for not disclosing my condition as I did not look for sympathy and never wanted any excuse to shirk work. Her affectionate words of encouragement, 'Ma'am, *aapki himmat ka jawab nahin*,' made me sail through. She even offered financial assistance. 'Ma'am, *main* ATM card *lekar aayi hoon*. If I may...' She also did not know how to put across her sentiments and feelings.

'Neeraja, not required. I am touched by your gesture. Husband *hain*, sister *hain*, *phir tumne* CGHS card *bhi banwa diya hain*. Thanks,' I had replied.

Her overall concern and care were reflected in every word she spoke, and in all her actions. Neeraja, I have no words to thank you.

Another colleague, then an additional CIT, Munish Kumar, helped a lot. He very promptly forwarded my representation to the Central Board of Direct Taxes, New Delhi, for retention in Bhopal after my promotion which was due.

He got my leave sanctioned for surgery and visited me often. His conversations about it being God's will and one should embrace a path of spirituality in life comforted me. He included me in his prayers. He initiated me into chanting the *mahamantra* which in turn took away all fear, tension and restlessness, and I completely surrendered myself to God. I became a person who was now geared up to take on the rough journey which was in the offing–surgery, eight chemos at an interval of fifteen days, twenty-five radiotherapy sessions and the follow-up check-ups and tests. He suggested Dr T.P. Sahu, who is a thorough professional. Under Dr Sahu I could go through all my chemos successfully. Munish, on a number of occasions, accompanied me to meet Dr Sahu and was there for any assistance. Whenever I thanked him, he was very humble and modest about it and refused to take any credit for his kind gesture.

Vikas Rakheja is my friend of more than fifteen years. He is also my publisher. He was one of the first persons to know of my illness. I clearly remember the day when I gave him a call and asked him to come to my office in the afternoon.

'Anything urgent, Madam?'

'*Aap aa jana*', I replied.

He came at 12 o'clock. I ordered coffee and told my peon not to send in any visitors.

'I have been diagnosed with malignancy. I have to go to Delhi for detailed investigations to be followed by surgery the day after,' I said in a very composed voice.

He was shocked, 'When did this happen?'

'It was diagnosed on Friday. You are one amongst the very few to know,' my voice cracked and I could barely hold back tears.

'You have to fight it for your daughter and I am sure you can do it,' were his encouraging words.

He added, 'Everything will be fine. Now it's a highly curable disease. Santosh along with the vehicle will be there in Delhi. I will instruct him to report to you from this moment onwards,'

His words that I have to live for my Chini motivated

me. The mother in me turned into a brave person who had to survive, come what may. Vikas's magical words gave me the strength to move ahead. Having been one of the biggest publishers of motivational books, he had imbibed all the positivity he could to inspire and encourage me.

The next morning he sent me a copy of *Magic* with a note. Vikas is the one who gave me the confidence that I was capable of putting up a fight. I decided, 'Begin now.' There was no need to languish but the need of the hour was to learn that the sun sets in the evening to rise again the next morning.

When I was returning from Delhi after my initial check-up, I met Vikas at the airport. My fifth book, *Until You Come Home,* was in the final stages and was to go for printing shortly.

'We will have a grand launch for the book. Whatever you say, wherever you say. These tough times will pass soon.' By talking about my forthcoming book, he gave me another hope and a dream.

Until You Come Home was launched with big fanfare at Marriot, Bhopal. It was attended by the media, all my friends and colleagues. This was followed by a function at Lucknow in November 2018. It was organised by my friend of more than twenty years, Mr Chander Prakash, of Universal Book Sellers. A question-answer session and interaction with the Press was also organised. The event had a huge press coverage. A book-reading session was also organised in Crossword bookstore in Treasure Island Next, Indore. This was also attended by a large number of book enthusiasts and, again, the event was a huge success. Another interactive session was organised by Club Literati at the Arera Club, Bhopal, in January 2019. The event was beautifully compered by Kena Shree, a well-known anchor from Delhi. I am happy that despite the tough and trying times I was able to create something nice. The credit for this goes to my friend and publisher, Vikas Rakheja.

His wife Anu-ji is a gem of a human being. She has always been very nice and sweet to all of us. She did not know of my illness. Her affectionate and caring nature is something to be remembered and cherished.

Recently I came across an excellent review of *Until You Come Home* by Swapna Peri in the December 2019 issue of the *Storizen* Magazine. She wrote:

The book, *Until You Come Home: The Endless Wait for a Beloved to Come Home from War,* is emotional and elusive. It is about war tales, family and its emotions, sentiments and memories about lost ones. The book emphasises mostly on the women and children of soldiers who lost their lives in wars fighting for the country. This tear-jerking novel is narrated in a single voice of Mrinalini Sharma. The story is about Mrinalini's Mama, Captain Uday Sharma. Jaya, the lady love of Uday Sharma, keeps waiting for him even after the news he will not come back home is one of the most heart-wrenching subplots. Another story is about Mrinalani herself and her partner Dev, who is also an army officer. When he is posted to Kargil, her thoughts and fears are narrated in the story. Two parallel stories are narrated where they are interlinked at several places.

As praises and salutes pour in for the brave army personnel who safeguard the country standing on the borders without bothering about the rough terrain and unfavourable climatic conditions, their families wait for a single look. It is indeed very hard to explain how a newly-wed woman or parents or children feel when they hear the news of the army person missing or dead.

In this book, the author has explained such sequences blended with two parallel stories where one is a tragic one and the other, a realistic one. This book is a powerful novel about the unexpected lives of army people. One of the standing points in the story is the female character, Mrinalini, who narrates the story about her Mama, Captain Uday Sharma, who never came back after he was sent to fight the Chinese Army at Sela Pass, in the 1962 war with China. She has never seen him but just heard about him. It is a common practice that since childhood, kids in the houses are told about the tales of great people who hail from the family itself. And thus, Mrinalini is enchanted with her Mama's valour and discipline.

Mrinalini who looks up to her Mama because of his duty and dedication towards the country, on the contrary, is apprehensive when her beau Dev, being from the army, is posted at Kargil during war. Here, the author Mridula very honestly explains how all kinds of thoughts torture the brave hearts of the family and create a gloomy situation.

What I liked:

1. The plot and the narration are beautifully crafted.
2. One can relate it to the recent incidents and movies that showcased how a family gets affected when a soldier leaves the world.
3. Heart-wrenching scenes are illustrated leaving a cold feeling in the readers' minds.
4. The brave hearts of the family members of the martyrs leave a heavy feeling in the minds.
5. The comfortable font size and paragraph styling.

What I didn't like:

There is nothing to be disliked.

Characters:

Every character is sketched so well and coherently.

Narration:

I have come across one of the finest and honest narrations in this book.

Language and Grammar:

With simple language and vocabulary, the book is suitable for everyone.

My Final Verdict:

An immensely touching story.
Book Title: 4/5
Book Cover: 4/5
Plot: 4/5
Characters: 4/5
Narration: 4/5
Language and Grammar: 4/5
Final Rating: 4/5

Eleven

A big debate goes around alternative therapies like Reiki, homeopathy, ayurveda, acupuncture, Tibetan and others versus allopathy. I opted for traditional allopathic treatment, i.e., surgery followed by chemotherapy and then radiotherapy, followed by regular check-ups, blood tests, yearly mammography tests, bone density tests, etc. The success rate and side effects of allopathic treatment are recorded, quantifiable and measurable. The medical history of such cases is easily accessible. Alternative therapy, I personally feel, is fine only after one is through with traditional therapy. This is purely my personal opinion though. Many have not been able to successfully fight the illness when they relied totally on alternative therapies.

Now I take alternative treatment as a follow-up—moringa powder, wheatgrass powder, organic turmeric, cinnamon powder, pepper, etc., are used on a regular basis. I take a glass of lemon water the first thing every morning. I started with these three months after the last chemo session was over. It is not known whether these alternate therapies interfere with allopathic treatment. However, the side effects of my follow-up medicines like Femera, Osteofos and Rockbon are insignificant. All the three-monthly blood tests like CBP, LFT, RFT, etc., are normal. The yearly tests conducted to check Thyroid, D_3, cholesterol levels, etc., are all fine. I owe a lot to these alternative herbal medicines/supplements as a follow-up routine.

I strictly adhered to certain 'Don'ts' which in turn helped me greatly. I suggest if one believes in them, they in turn make one sail through.

1. Do not think about the illness.
2. Discuss about it only with the doctor or someone who has first-hand knowledge/information about it.
3. Read as little as possible about the illness over the internet. By reading too much one only gets stress and tension.
4. Count your blessings and lead a normal life. When the side effects of chemo are reduced, try doing household chores. I even cooked food and made tea in the week after the chemo session.

There is a list of 'Do's' that I made and I wish to share them.

1. Have faith in God for He is kind and merciful.
2. Pray daily.
3. Help all you see around you as far as possible. The law of nature is that each one gives and receives. Those who do not, have an empty heart and soul.
4. Build your emotional account. Let people know that you are grateful for what they do and speak. It's equally important to have a support network.

We all need people who care about us and can help us to get back on track when we have lost our way.

Luck comes to you when destiny eventually gets tired of waiting. I felt the need to understand the joy of giving.

The important question that I ask, 'What are you doing to make others happy? What are you doing to ease the pain of others?'

You pass this way but once, so fill your life with a lot of helping acts.

Nature gives us in abundance and one can learn from it. We receive so much without giving anything in return. Now was the time to try and do something for someone who can never repay. It's wonderful to bring light in the dark corner of someone's life.

I appreciate the importance of love. Love has no reason and this life is too short for wasting it on petty things. I am surrounded by the love of all my dear ones. I pray to God that my body gets stronger and healthier day by day. I learnt to love myself and look forward to miracles in my life.

Now I am cured and healed. I thank God for all I have. Always thank all those who held your hand during these tough days. Recall happy and pleasant moments of life. Always believe in fairy-tales. There is romance in life. Birds sing and stars fall from the blazing sky.

One should never stop being a good person because of bad people. Always forgive all who have done wrong to you. Remember when you forgive you heal. When you let go of things that have made you unhappy, you recover. I forgive all who may have hurt me and I let go of all negative thoughts. It is important to be kind to others.

Twelve

I have summed up my struggle and my fight, from manuscript to print. It's a portrayal of how a woman has to largely make her own efforts to survive and secure her tomorrow. As I look back and remember life, I recall the number of times I longed to change the world for the better in small, small ways. Many a times I was disappointed. But I am happy that I tried. As a woman I say (for I cannot preach or demand) that a woman should always try hard to live her own life on her own terms even while playing the role of a mother, a wife, a daughter, a sister or a friend.

Never give up because you see so many unhappy endings for women all around. Life may not always have a fairy-tale ending but life is an amazing story by itself. It shows various beautiful shades–kindness, trust, love and the satisfaction of giving and helping.

I am fortunate that I tried and I am happy that I longed to change the world for the better. I saw life at its best and also survived it when it went downhill. It has taught me so much. There were roses, balloons, cotton candies, ice-cream, chocolates and, many a times, bitter coffee that I gradually learnt to relish. The important lesson I learnt is one should never give up hope and one's pursuit of happiness. When life gets tougher, try to be your own hero. And, finally, after two years, I decided to put down my story.

Living through such tough times and surviving was wonderful. I realised how beautiful and such a blessing life is each day, each month and each year that we live. One should appreciate each moment of life. Life is a great gift of God. I thank Him for every moment. The good and the bad, some were blessings and some were lessons.

Today is very important and what we do today is what matters most. Life must be tied to some goal. In these two years, I realised that difficult paths always take one to beautiful destinations. I also learnt that it is impossible to undo the past but one can learn and understand it and try not to spend any moment in future in regret, fear or guilt. Many times life is not perfect but it never ceases to be beautiful.

A line that inspired me and has been my life's motto since then, and I follow it to the earnest:

'Learn from yesterday, live for today, hope for tomorrow.'

God's grace is important. Life does not work without God's grace as it is immeasurable and it is faith in God and His miracle that made me go on. He opened so many doors for me. Problems came from one direction but help poured in from so many other quarters.

As I had surrendered to God's will, it gave me the serenity to accept the harsh times. I was very sure of God's help and it is very true that by thinking positive one always attracts positive outcomes. Try and attract good things in life. I try and interact with people who are positive, happy and contended.

I have been through several bad days. I realised that whenever life went downhill for me, God intervened and pulled me back. Providential help was around the corner. I don't know to what I owe this. The blessings of my elders, the good deeds of my ancestors, the prayers of my mother, the good I had done, the good luck of Chini, my princess, or the love of my husband or something else? I cannot summarise but it was always there.

All that was painful, unpleasant is over. Now life is back on track and I am confident that tomorrow will bring happiness.

I did my work, achieved my annual targets, I even sat through lengthy conferences and edited the first Hindi magazine for the office. God was kind that none of the conferences fell on the day of my chemotherapy sessions.

I learnt that happiness comes from within. They were tough times–the diagnosis, surgery, chemo, radio, chemo port flushing, regular check-ups, blood tests, constantly being watched and monitored. Yet life is beautiful and full of dreams. I have to live long and see so many things–Chini excelling in her work, her painting exhibition, her settling down in life, my mother growing older and my sister and I growing old along with her; my husband picking up ranks.

My motto in life is 'The best is yet to come', and I always hope for a better tomorrow.

My Mother's Story...

I am sure everyone will like to listen to my mother's story as it only lives on if there are people willing to listen.

I prevailed upon my mother to write, else the story would have remained inside her, untold. She was diagnosed with Stage 2b breast cancer in September 2017. My mother has narrated two years of her ordeal from diagnosis, surgery, followed by eight chemo sessions and twenty-five radiotherapy sessions, not to forget the follow-up check-ups. That was not the end. There were still three monthly and yearly check-ups, the monthly flushing of the chemo port and, finally, its surgical removal after two years. She has written about these months so that others can be motivated and inspired to fight this deadly disease.

Many would have heard such a story before, but

don't stop me. You may find something new here that you may decide to narrate to someone in future. I hope the story inspires and motivates.

One question that always perturbed me was, 'Why my mother?'

There is no answer.

When cancer strikes a dear one, the entire family breaks down and when you love someone, the fear of losing that person haunts you.

The day her hair went I cried and when she lost seven of her nails, her eyelashes and eyebrows, I completely broke down. Nothing could console me.

It is often said that one is obliged to change one's name as one is no longer what one once was. My mother is a transformed person as she has come out of this. She is a survivor because her courage never left her and hope was always by her side. To live through hard times, one needs sturdy support. I am very thankful for our wonderful family. She could survive the illness and we could sail through it because of our family. No one has a perfect family but it is a great feeling to have a united one. I can only say that having a family is everything. It was her strong will power, the support of the family and our faith in God that my mother is a survivor today.

I thank everyone who showed kindness and extended their support during these days. The journey through her illness was not easy but it gave me a better understanding of many things. Another thing that I would like to say is that life is so beautiful. Each day that we live is not magical, but there is some magic in each day. In order to live through tough times one has to be in love with life. I learnt to celebrate success and also what was not a success.

My philosophy towards life also changed. Life teaches us so much as it brings downfalls and harsh moments. I learnt a lesson, 'Remember your blessings and not your burdens.'

I analysed a big question, 'What can be done for others?'

'You pass this way but once,' is what I had been taught. So there was an urgent need to lend a helping hand to all who are in need of help.

My mother went for her annual check-up in March 2021 and was, thankfully, given a clean chit, thereby completing the three-year mark post receiving the last round of treatments.

I prayed to God earlier and I pray to Him now, and thank Him for giving a fairy-tale ending to our story, and for allowing us to live happily ever after.

Mrinalini Pandey